A Wedding Guide for Catholics

A Wedding Guide for Catholics

Planning a Wedding AND Thriving in Marriage

Nadine and Irv Brechner,
Peg Hensler, Paulette and John Pitonyak, and
Carol and Robert Schilling

Paulist Press
New York / Mahwah, NJ

Cover image by Andrei Ozhegov/Dreamstime.com
Cover and book design by Lynn Else

Nihil obstat:
Rev. Scott Shaffer
Pastor, St. Joseph Parish
Toms River, New Jersey

Imprimatur:
The Most Rev. David M. O'Connell, C.M., Th.M., J.C.D.
Bishop of Trenton
May 10, 2024

Library of Congress Cataloging-in-Publication Data
Names: Brechner, Irv, author.
Title: A wedding guide for Catholics: planning a wedding and thriving in marriage / Irv and Nadine Brechner, Peg Hensler, Paulette and John Pitonyak, and Carol and Robert Schilling.
Description: New York, Mahwah, NJ: Paulist Press, [2025] | Summary: "This book provides tools for a successful Catholic marriage"—Provided by publisher.
Identifiers: LCCN 2024036543 (print) | LCCN 2024036544 (ebook) | ISBN 9780809157235 (paperback) | ISBN 9780809188918 (ebook)
Subjects: LCSH: Marriage—Religious aspects—Catholic Church.
Classification: LCC BX2250 .B733 2025 (print) | LCC BX2250 (ebook) | DDC 234/.165—dc23/eng/20250111
LC record available at https://lccn.loc.gov/2024036543
LC ebook record available at https://lccn.loc.gov/2024036544

ISBN 978-0-8091-5723-5 (paperback)
ISBN 978-0-8091-8891-8 (ebook)

Published by Paulist Press
997 Macarthur Boulevard
Mahwah, NJ 07430
www.paulistpress.com

Printed and bound in the
United States of America

To our adult children—
from the day you came into our lives
to when you said, "I Do,"
you have been a great joy and source
of happiness and memorable milestones.

Nadine & Irv Brechner
Paulette & John Pitonyak
Carol & Bob Schilling

* * *

For my husband, Bob,
who supports me through every marriage ministry project,
is my color commentator for so many Pre-Cana events,
and who never stops encouraging me to
step out of my comfort zone;
and for all the engaged couples who
want the best marriage ever!

Peg Hensler

Contents

Contents

Part II. Survive: Relieving Stress

Contents

Part III. Thrive: The Future

Preface

A parishioner from a local parish, John Pitonyak, once contacted me and asked if I'd be interested in reviewing his book, *The Wedding Survival Kit.* Since I had never seen anything like it in all my thirty-five years of working with newly engaged couples, I agreed.

After reading it, I realized that his book had a tremendous amount of timely and helpful information, but it wasn't right for Catholics. So, I issued John a challenge: Would he like to create a Catholic version, combining what he'd already done, with additional Catholic content that would make the book perfect for couples around the world?

He gave a resounding and immediate positive response, and that's how we got started.

The result is *A Wedding Guide for Catholics*. This book will help couples enjoy a traditional Catholic wedding combined with secular celebrations. It's truly an essential guidebook for Catholics getting married today.

You will discover, in reading this book, what's important within the rich tradition of the Catholic wedding and how these elements are distinctive among the many other ways to celebrate a wedding.

You'll also find short passages from the Bible sprinkled throughout the book as they apply to specific sections on relieving stress.

Designed as an essential guidebook, *A Wedding Guide for Catholics* can be used throughout the wedding-planning process so that you minimize stress and enjoy the celebration.

Peg Hensler

Acknowledgments

We give special thanks to Rev. Jim Grogan, Rev. Bill Lago, and Rev. Scott Shaffer for their careful review of the book, their suggested revisions, and their exuberant support of this project. And to Rev. Robert Pagliari for his fine contribution.

Introduction

Congratulations to the engaged couple and their parents, family, and friends! The goal of this book is to make the wedding-planning process a joyous and fun experience for all.

The first section of the book is possibly the most important one. Read it carefully before you look at the two sections that follow.

After planning weddings with our adult children, we decided to write a book to help parents and couples have wonderfully positive experiences during this milestone life event and many others. We have condensed our experiences, research, and interviews with countless others into a roadmap to help you:

- reduce and minimize stress, conflict, and frustration;
- minimize problems so that the journey is smooth, fun, and joyful;
- create a special experience for your family in the digital age;
- make important, timely, and long-lasting decisions together;
- save money without sacrificing enjoyment.

On writing this book, we agreed that we wished there had been a book like this for when our adult children had told us they were getting married.

Having the right mindset is essential for engaged couples and parents and is the essence of this book.

WHO SHOULD READ THIS BOOK

This book is more than a wedding-planning guide for couples, parents, and grandparents. It's also for those who have had a major influence on the lives of the bride and groom and are sources of wisdom and guidance for the couple, including godparents, siblings, mentors, and special friends. In fact, anyone who wants the best possible marriage for their loved ones should read this book.

USING THIS BOOK

There are different ways to get the most out of this book. Reading it from cover to cover is *not* one of them. You'll find some intentional repetition because the book has been written so that *everyone*—couples, parents, and even grandparents—can remove the stress and help make the big day successful.

First, when the couple announces their engagement, you might scan the table of contents and read the first stress reducer, "Having a Vision." When children tell their parents that they are getting married, one of the first things parents are eager to do, aside from congratulating the couple, is to learn about the couple's vision for the wedding, whenever they are ready...but the sooner the better.

A second suggestion is to read individual stress reducers as specific situations come up. So, when you want to talk about compiling the invitation list, read stress reducer 13, "Whom to Invite" so that you can speak specifically about the topic and avoid problems before they arise.

Finally, there are some general sections like the one you're reading now that you may want to read several times to keep our recommended principles in mind.

CLOSE COLLABORATION

We've observed that the most successful weddings have been the result of a close collaboration between the bride and groom and between the engaged couple and their parents. The almost unanimous observations among those who loved their weddings include:

- parents do not *always* need to "suck it up" and do whatever the couple wants;
- parents should never *demand* certain things because they are paying for all or part of the wedding;
- couples should sincerely take their parents' wishes into consideration and try to incorporate them while maintaining their vision of the wedding day.

The best approach is for everyone to put aside the "it's all about us" attitude and learn how to compromise and talk things through so everyone can enjoy the wedding.

PROACTIVE CONVERSATIONS

Whether you are talking about planning a wedding or a myriad of issues that all couples face, the best way to deal with these situations is by having a frank and honest conversation.

So, when children announce their engagement, approach the couple about having a proactive conversation so that together the couple and parents can make the wedding special. Recognize the importance of truly understanding what the happy couple wants and doesn't want.

The worst approach is to wait for a conflict to arise. Talk about it sooner than later so that everyone can consider what is best for all and understand the vision for the wedding day.

THE FUN OF COMPROMISE

When thinking about invitations, we (Nadine and Irv) wanted ours to look like a personal ad in a newspaper, resembling how we met, but we realized that more traditional people—like our parents—would prefer something a little less quirky.

So we compromised by having two invitations—one for older folks and the personal ad version for our friends and younger adults. People are still talking about our personal ad invitation many years later, and our parents really appreciated the traditional version.

AN OUTSIDE-THE-BOX APPROACH

If you are anticipating facing many conflicts, potentially major ones, it might be worth considering a different approach. We call this "veto rights," and, while it may not be for everyone, in some cases it might work.

In these situations the engaged couple and both sets of parents each get one veto, or the couple gets two and the parents one each, or whatever you decide. When an issue arises and, after talking it through, there's still no agreement, one party can use their "veto right." For example, in deciding on the music for the reception, one group may veto having a band in favor of a DJ. Of course, it is wise to try to resolve as many issues as possible and save the veto for issues that really matter. This specific method levels the playing field and gives everyone a means to get their "nonnegotiables."

Part I

STRIVE

Initial Planning

The Wedding Ceremony

Having now covered many of the basics, let's consider the joy and glory of a wedding ceremony that can be summarized as the three *Ms*:

- Majestic
- Memorable
- Meaningful

Whether the ceremony is celebrated in a charming small church, like the mountaintop chapel in the movie *Mamma Mia*, or in a grand church with stained-glass windows and a pipe organ, or anything in-between, it will be majestic, memorable, and meaningful for the couple. It may also be miraculous, especially when you comprehend the profound positive impact that faith and a church ceremony can have, not only for the wedding day but for the entire marriage.

The rich tradition of the Catholic wedding ceremony is very beautiful and special. The Catholic wedding usually takes place in the church and is truly a sacred covenant. The Catholic Church does make exceptions to this custom in particular circumstances. You should discuss how flexible your local diocese is, with the priest, deacon, or marriage coordinator helping you to prepare for your wedding.

In situations where both the bride and the groom are Catholic, you need to decide how important a traditional Catholic wedding ceremony is to you and then plan accordingly.

Part I: Strive

While you can leave the technical aspects of your marriage preparation to experts like your priest or a deacon, a basic understanding of the marriage preparation and wedding-planning process in the Church is important so that you can make the best decisions possible. You'll read some "churchy" terms, but we have kept definitions relatively simple.

General Perspectives

A Catholic wedding ceremony reflects the couple's commitment to their faith. While the reception is the occasion to showcase their unique personalities, the ceremony is about tradition, sacredness, and liturgical ritual, which transcend time.

While some venues promote the convenience of having the wedding ceremony and reception under one roof, it is the wedding ceremony (or Mass) that is the primary focus of the day. If both the bride and groom are Catholic, a nuptial Mass taking place in a Catholic church is an appropriate choice.

In some dioceses, Catholic wedding ceremonies without a Mass may be celebrated with permission at approved non-church sites or reception venues. Check with your priest or deacon to find out whether this is acceptable.

When working with their parish to plan their wedding, couples may hear two different terms regarding their Catholic ceremony: *nuptial* and *liturgy*. *Nuptial* is simply another word for wedding or marriage; *liturgy* refers to the ceremony in church. A Catholic wedding liturgy can be a full nuptial Mass with holy communion or a nuptial ceremony that includes prayers, scripture readings, and the exchange of vows. Your priest or deacon can explain the difference further.

A Catholic marriage is foremost about the couple forming a permanent bond of love that will nurture their nuclear and extended families; it is also deeply connected to the Catholic faith community. Ideally, you want the wedding to take place at your parish church.

For weddings, parishes typically require a donation that covers the use of the church, the musicians or cantors, and other expenses that may be incurred by the parish.

When planning a Catholic wedding, it may seem as if the parish is just like any other wedding vendor; just like everyone else, they want you to have the wedding of your dreams. But consider the difference: wedding vendors, on the one hand, are there for you throughout the months of wedding planning. Their goal is to meet or exceed your expectations for a wonderful wedding experience. Once they fulfill their contracts and ask you for a positive online review, the relationship is basically over.

Your parish, on the other hand, is your faith community, a constant throughout your lives supporting you through every milestone of your marriage and family life, in good times and bad, in sickness and in health, much like your own marital relationship.

Your parish will always be there for you, and your marriage and family life are strengthened by your full participation in the Catholic faith community—a lifelong relationship for the good of all.

Preparation Basics

There are three things that need to be done once a couple is engaged: set the date, review the situation, and prepare.

Set the date. Now that you're engaged, contact your church as soon as possible, ideally a year or so before your desired wedding date. Do this yourself. Many dioceses typically require at least six months or up to a year of preparation for a Catholic marriage. Reception venues may need to be booked up to two years in advance. In such cases, once the reception venue is booked, you should notify the parish so that the wedding date can be reserved.

Review the situation. The priest or deacon who will be preparing you for marriage will conduct a review of your unique situation to ensure that it will be a valid Catholic marriage. He will walk you through the process and the steps to be completed.

Prepare. Parishes will work with you to complete a customized preparation process, typically involving private sessions, participation in a Pre-Cana program, and possibly working with a Catholic mentor couple who will accompany you throughout this process and into the early years of marriage.

There are several important issues surrounding what are commonly called valid and sacramental weddings: a wedding may either be valid *and* sacramental or valid but *not* sacramental.

People often think a valid marriage is also a sacrament, but this isn't so. If you're unsure of how your pending marriage will be viewed by the Church, consult your priest or deacon for a complete explanation.

The sacrament of marriage is an outward sign of the exchange of marital consent on the part of a baptized man and a baptized woman. The officiant—the priest or deacon—does not marry the couple; the couple marries each other.

The Three C's

A marriage that is recognized by the Catholic Church has three components: capacity, consent, and canonical form.

Capacity is the ability to live a Catholic marriage. This requires maturity and the willingness to love and honor each other until death. To proceed, couples must be "free"—no prior marriages, holy orders, or religious vows. A prior marriage must have been annulled, which declares that it was not valid.

Consent requires full understanding and agreement without reservation that a Catholic marriage is permanent and cannot be dissolved. Furthermore, the couple must be faithful to each other and God and be willing to have children.

Canonical form is based on the canon law of the Roman Catholic Church. It defines the elements necessary for the wedding Mass or ceremony to be valid. This includes the actions and words of the rite of marriage—the official prayers, promises, and rituals of Catholic marriage—and that the marriage takes place in a Catholic church. Canonical form also requires that the official witness of the Church, the officiant, be a priest or deacon in good standing. The presence of two legal witnesses—traditionally the "best man" and "maid or matron of honor"—is also required. Any change in this canonical form requires a dispensation (special permission for a non-Catholic ceremony).

In certain circumstances, a dispensation from canonical form can be requested when a Catholic marries a non-Catholic or unbaptized person.

The Wedding Rehearsal

The wedding rehearsal is a very important part of the process. It's an opportunity to prepare the couple, their families, and the wedding party for their roles in the wedding Mass or ceremony and to explain the significance of the wedding liturgy—how the ritual unfolds.

Rehearsals often represent the "coming home" of Catholics who have been away from the Church for some time. They offer a great opportunity for those to reconnect and renew their commitment to their faith, and for the celebrant—the priest or deacon—to pray with the couple and wedding party.

You may consider asking your celebrant or priest of your parish to offer the sacrament of reconciliation to you and any Catholic members of your wedding party at the conclusion of the rehearsal or in the days prior to your wedding.

If there are family members or guests who don't get along—because of divorce, acrimonious relationships, and so on—you should disclose this to the priest or deacon prior to the rehearsal so that appropriate seating arrangements for the wedding Mass or ceremony can be made. This can prevent uncomfortable surprises at the church that could ruin the wedding day (see chapter 15, "Making Demands," in part 2).

The Wedding Day

Traditionally there are three days of the week on which Catholic weddings can take place, each with different circumstances; however, every parish is different, so check with the parish first.

Saturday daytime. The wedding would typically be no later than 2:00 p.m. due to parish confessions and/or Saturday evening Mass. If there is a significant gap between the ceremony and reception, you should plan activities and food for your guests.

Friday evening. Typically, the ceremony will be followed by the reception at a venue.

Sunday afternoon. While some parishes offer Sundays, you should realize that Sundays are the busiest days at the church, and the wedding cannot interfere with Masses, social activities, and baptisms. If the wedding falls on a Sunday, the correct practice is to use the Sunday readings rather than those recommended for Catholic weddings, but check with your local parish.

Weekdays (Monday–Thursday). In some cases couples can request a weekday wedding. This could be due to a family health issue or such things as the reception taking place in a foreign country or if the couple is already civilly married. In this situation, decisions are made by the individual parish.

The Wedding Day Schedule

The most beautiful and memorable weddings are those that not only honor the sacredness of marriage but also give every participant, from the bride and groom to their families and friends, the wedding banquet that God intends for us—a true feast.

In planning your wedding day, let's consider a typical scenario. The day often begins with the bride and her attendants coming together several hours before the ceremony for the communal ritual of getting hair and makeup done and helping the bride with her wedding gown.

The groom and groomsmen may also get together as a show of support for the husband-to-be. Keep in mind that no alcohol can be consumed within five hours of the ceremony. That's because the bride and groom must come to the ceremony 100 percent alert so that there is no doubt as to the intent for lifelong commitment.

Let's say the wedding Mass is scheduled to begin at 1:00 p.m. and the reception begins at 5:00 p.m. Allowing an hour for the Mass, followed by time for a reception line and for guests to greet one another outside the church, there will be at least two hours between the wedding and the reception.

To make the day truly special, it's important to plan pre-reception activities for your guests—perhaps a family member or two who live near the church will offer to host a gathering with snacks and soft drinks. If pre-reception parties can't accommodate all guests, the bride and groom can post various ideas for enjoying the time before the reception.

Suggested activities could include visiting a local tavern, taking a walk about town, or visiting a local park. In planning events for your wedding guests, they will feel valued and enjoy their time together.

After enjoying the pre-reception events, it's time for everyone to gather for the great feast. This might begin with a cocktail hour and include special toasts to the bride and groom, followed by dinner and dancing, and then perhaps an afterparty at the venue, hotel, or another location. It is important to plan well for all wedding day events to ensure the best results.

A Nuptial Mass or Ceremony

If most guests are not practicing Catholics and, therefore, not able to participate fully in a Mass, the couple might consider a nuptial ceremony instead. Here are some important points to note:

- For Catholic weddings, the nuptial/wedding Mass or nuptial ceremony is the most important part of the day and should be carefully planned by the couple with the assistance of the priest, deacon, or perhaps a wedding coordinator of the parish.
- When it comes to music, parishes often have guidelines, providing many beautiful songs to choose from. If you wish to bring in your own musicians or have a friend or family member sing, they should have some experience with Catholic weddings. Beautiful music brings great joy and makes the wedding more memorable.
- In planning the ceremony, you can give special roles to important people in your lives. These roles include readers or lectors—for the first and second readings, petitions/Prayer of the Faithful—and if there is a Mass, gift bearers (those who will bring up the gifts at the Offertory), eucharistic ministers, and altar servers.

- The readings you select and those who read them can make a huge difference to the beauty and solemnity of the liturgy. Readers should be well spoken and should familiarize themselves with the passages, as they will be proclaiming the Word of God.
- You have the option to customize the petitions/ the Prayer of the Faithful to include causes that are important to you and the congregation. Ask your priest or deacon about what is appropriate.
- There are four appropriate items to consider regarding the procession and greeting of the guests, and you should arrange this section in whatever way makes you feel most comfortable:

    - Since the wedding is about the couple and not just the bride, it is appropriate for both to greet guests prior to the ceremony, if they wish to do so.
    - Because the wedding is about the blending of two families, the procession may begin with the groom and his parents, the bridal party, and finally the bride with her parents.
    - Another option is for the bride and groom to enter together, with the parents of both included in the procession, along with the bridal party, readers, and the priest or deacon.
    - While it is most popular for the father to give away the bride, adhering to this tradition may not adequately reflect the equal partnership of husband and wife. Perhaps a more appropriate option is for the bride to be accompanied by her father and mother.

Interfaith Weddings

Catholic and Jewish, Catholic and Muslim, and Catholic and unbaptized weddings, among others, can take place in a church-reception venue or some other neutral nonreligious site and should honor the traditions of both faiths. In this chapter, we will consider the example of a Catholic/Jewish interfaith wedding.

Since Jewish families and guests may feel uncomfortable in a Catholic church, it is appropriate to combine both Jewish and Catholic rites in a respectful outdoor ceremony, which is a common location for many Jewish weddings. At Peg's daughter's wedding, for example, the officiants talked about the Judeo-Christian tradition as a sacred covenant. They also explained the following religious traditions that may have been unfamiliar to some people in attendance:

- In the Christian tradition, the cross is the ultimate sign of God's self-giving love, a reminder that married love is given freely, totally, faithfully, and forever. The vertical beam of the cross points to heaven and symbolizes our singular relationship with God. The horizontal beam symbolizes that we are all connected as one human family.
- In the Jewish tradition, the ketubah is the "firm and binding" document or standard marriage contract that Jewish law requires a groom to provide for his bride on their wedding day, a sacred promise to "cherish, honor, protect, and sustain" each other. The chuppah is the wedding canopy

that symbolizes the physical and spiritual home created together. The breaking of the glass is a symbolic reminder of the loss of the temple in Jerusalem and the fragility of life. It's an exuberant cue for the celebration to begin, as family and friends call out, "Mazel tov!"

THE STORY OF A BEAUTIFUL INTERFAITH WEDDING

This story is told by Peg Hensler and is an example of how one small detail can potentially derail an entire wedding. In this case, it was the wedding of Peg's Catholic daughter and her future Jewish son-in-law. The rabbi and priest had already arrived at the venue where the outdoor portion of the wedding would take place under the chuppah according to Jewish tradition.

This ceremony was a blend of two faith traditions, and all items used for the wedding ritual were chosen due to their special significance. Everything was falling nicely into place—the florist was finalizing the flowers for the chuppah, and the other items were being arranged appropriately.

A large wooden cross about five feet tall—not a crucifix, which bears the image of Christ's body and would present a problem for the Jewish family and guests—was to be set off to the side as a Christian symbol of sacrificial love. The cross was mistakenly placed immediately behind the chuppah, which upset the rabbi to the point where she would not perform the ceremony unless it was moved.

For my husband and me, the Catholic parents of the bride, we wanted to dig in our heels and keep the cross nearby. We felt that we had already made many concessions, but our daughter begged us to move the cross so it would not be part of the wedding ceremony. For the sake of our daughter, we quickly relented.

In the end, the sacred ceremony blended the faith traditions more beautifully than we could have imagined. To this day, people still tell us that it was their favorite wedding ceremony—the perfect reflection of our daughter and son-in-law's new interfaith family. With miscommunication and stubbornness, we could have ruined our daughter's wedding, but instead it has become one of our most treasured memories.

Destination Weddings

Some wedding destinations—such as the mountaintop church in the movie *Mamma Mia*—are acceptable alternatives to Catholic churches. You can find churches and chapels at many beautiful island resorts or in other countries whose priests or deacons can validly officiate the ceremony. If you are planning a destination wedding, work with your local Catholic parish and their diocesan canonical services office to make sure all the paperwork is handled properly, even if the wedding isn't in a church on a mountaintop. Consider the following pertinent points:

- The local diocese may give special permission in exceptional cases to hold the ceremony at the reception site or other location.
- Couples who wish to hold all wedding-related events on one date at the reception site can request a Catholic wedding, perhaps with minimal family and two witnesses, prior to the full wedding celebration. This wedding ceremony should be held in a church and could take place days, weeks, or even months in advance, and all marriage preparation and wedding arrangements must occur according to the usual Catholic requirements.
- Note that a wedding ceremony held by a Catholic couple at a reception site after the Catholic wedding has taken place is a *renewal* (reaffirmation) of vows. Only one legally binding and

valid Catholic wedding can take place. Catholic couples will often use their renewal ceremony as an opportunity to include special songs, poems, and nonscripture sacred readings that would not be appropriate for their Catholic wedding ceremony.

Remarriage in the Church

The intentions for couples on their wedding day is that their marriage will last "all the days of their lives," but the reality is that Catholic marriages may end in divorce.

When a Catholic who is divorced finds love again and desires to marry in the Catholic Church, he or she, in consultation with their priest or deacon, may seek a declaration of nullity (an annulment). They may find that the marriage was not valid from the start (i.e., something was lacking in the capacity or consent for permanent and faithful marriage). The annulment process is often the catalyst for healing, forgiveness, and growth, which allows the person to move on from the prior relationship and give him- or herself fully to a new spouse in marriage.

For divorced Catholics whose prior marriage was outside the Church (not a valid Catholic marriage), a declaration of nullity is still needed, but the request is called a "lack of form" case, a straightforward process that requires a "petition for a decree of nullity" based on the absence of canonical form.

If a declaration of nullity is granted, that person is free to marry in the Catholic Church and will undergo marriage preparation that considers the additional complexity of family systems and any healing still needed. The Church recognizes the legality of prior marriages, so any children from those marriages are considered legitimate. To ensure that the new marriage will not be affected by unhealthy behaviors from the past, couples entering remarriage may wish to seek premarital counseling in addition to thorough marriage preparation in the Church.

A BRAND-NEW START

Your Catholic remarriage is a sacred and holy relationship like any first-time marriage. It is up to you as a couple, keeping in mind any blended family issues, to decide how your marriage will be celebrated. There are no rules in the Church that require an understated celebration of marriage because you were married before.

With careful sacramental preparation, prayer, the sacrament of reconciliation, and proper assistance from your parish, your wedding ceremony (or wedding Mass) and reception will be a perfect reflection of your loving relationship, with special consideration for all parties involved. By becoming actively involved in your parish, attending Mass regularly, and seeking the support of your parish community when needed, your marriage will be a blessing to all.

CONVALIDATION

Perhaps marriage in the Catholic Church was not important to you when you were first engaged, or perhaps there were circumstances that led you to have a civil marriage outside the Church. Whatever the reason, God desires for you to have a lifelong, grace-filled, happy marriage.

Once you decide together to bring your marriage to the next level, the first step is to notify your parish that you desire a Catholic marriage—that you both want your civil marriage to be recognized as valid in the Catholic Church (convalidation), and that you want to return to the other sacraments, especially the Eucharist.

As with regular, first-time marriages, you will begin the marriage preparation process at the parish with a prenuptial investigation (review) with your priest or deacon, and you will be required to complete sacramental education that may involve instructional sessions at the parish, a premarital inventory, working with a mentor couple and doing a marriage readiness retreat.

THE WEDDING CEREMONY

In the past, it was common for couples who were married before a justice of the peace, a civil judge, or a minister of another Christian church to plan a simple wedding ceremony with a small gathering of family and friends, followed by a low-key celebration.

For various reasons, with many couples choosing to postpone their big wedding celebration but not their legal marriage, convalidation has become far more common and is now being treated as any first-time Catholic marriage with the same marriage preparation and wedding planning process.

Making your civil marriage valid within the Church is cause for great celebration for you as a couple, and for your families, friends, and the Catholic faith community. Just as with all regular first-time marriages, a Mass is appropriate if both participants are Catholic, but if not, a nuptial ceremony may be better. All regular permissions apply, and your parish will assist you with your wedding plans.

Planning Your Wedding Ceremony

The following questions have been grouped into helpful sections denoting each stage of the process so that couples and their families can easily consider them as they prepare for their wedding day.

CONTACTING A PARISH

- How do you choose a parish for your wedding?
- Whom do you contact at the parish?
- What is the interview about?
- What are the fees?
- What paperwork and forms need to be filled out?

PREPARING FOR A LIFELONG MARRIAGE

- What are the requirements for marriage preparation?
- What are premarriage inventories?
- What marriage preparation programs are there?
- What is natural family planning (NFP)?

SETTING THE WEDDING DATE

- What dates should we avoid?
- What days are not allowed?
- What dates should we consider?

THE FORM OF YOUR WEDDING

- Who will preside at the wedding?
- What are "Catholic wedding priest" ads, and what should you know?
- What's the Order of Celebrating Matrimony within a Mass?
- What's the Order of Celebrating Matrimony without a Mass?
- What's the Order of Celebrating Matrimony between a Catholic and a catechumen or a non-Christian?

THE SCRIPTURE READINGS

- What are the options for the readings?
- Who do we want to perform the readings?
- What message is being proclaimed in the readings you choose?

THE WEDDING MUSIC

- Who at the parish can assist us with our music?
- What are the criteria for choosing Catholic wedding music?
- How do we find good musicians?

- At what stages of the wedding liturgy can we have music?
- What is the message of the songs, hymns, and other music we choose?

THE WEDDING VOWS

- Can we write our own Catholic wedding vows?
- Can we state intentions before the vows?
- Are there different versions of the vows we can choose?
- Do we need to memorize the vows?
- Should we have a song or acclamation after the vows?

THE ROLES FOR FAMILY AND FRIENDS

- bride and groom
- presider
- witnesses
- the wedding party
- assembly
- ushers
- musicians
- lectors (readers)
- extraordinary ministers of Holy Communion
- gift bearers
- altar servers
- flower girls and ring bearers

OTHER LITURGICAL ELEMENTS

- Is there a special way to greet guests?
- What should we know about seating?
- How should we greet the assembly?
- Who should be in the wedding procession?
- What are the Prayers of the Faithful?
- What prayers and blessings should we include?
- Should we have a unity candle at the ceremony or reception?
- Can we include a prayer to the Virgin Mary?

THE WEDDING PROGRAM

- How do we plan and create the wedding program?
- What are the options for creating and printing our Catholic wedding programs?
- Does our wedding program encourage participation?
- Should the program include the service music?
- Are there Catholic wedding program templates?

Topics for Your Pastor*

Under the broad category of "things couples often don't think about when planning their weddings," here are ten important items that couples are strongly advised to consider or discuss with their pastor well in advance of their wedding rehearsal.

Guests with special needs. Inform the pastor of any guest who may have special needs and require assistance.

Seating. Discuss with the pastor the seating arrangements for divorced parents.

Candles. Discuss the use of additional candles besides the candles on the altar. If the pastor permits additional candles, consider artificial candles, as they do not pose any hazards.

Rice or birdseed. Discuss with the pastor the use of rice or birdseed outside the church after the ceremony. Note that bubbles are another option.

Emotional support animals (ESAs). Churches have no prohibition against ESA-certified support animals. Discuss whether non-ESA animals are welcome at the ceremony.

White carpet runner. If you're using a runner, make sure that it's laid down before the start of the ceremony. Consider the potential hazards that having a runner presents for the guests.

Personal organist. Discuss if you prefer to have your own organist perform the music at your ceremony. If the church organist is salaried, this may not be an issue. If providing music

* Contributed by Rev. Robert Pagliari, CSsR, PhD, author of *Holy Homework* (New York: Catholic New York, 2018).

is an on-call hire, then you may have to pay a fee include the organist at the rehearsal for instructional purposes.

Alcohol. Remember that alcohol and marriage vows do not mix. Intoxication invalidates the requirement of free choice and full consent.

Rehearsal. To eliminate confusion during the wedding rehearsal and to honor the wishes of the couple, it is worth discussing the details of the ceremony with the priest or deacon prior to the rehearsal.

On-time arrivals and photo ops. Weddings usually occur on a Saturday. There are often time constraints due to Masses or Saturday confessions. Therefore, the bride and groom must be punctual.

Ask the priest or deacon for their policy regarding the photographer and videographer during the ceremony. If pictures or video recording is restricted during the ceremony, ask if it is possible to re-pose any significant moments afterward. If the priest or deacon is available, this may allow for a better photoshoot for lighting purposes and getting natural facial expressions. Most photographers agree that this is a less intrusive and far more professional option.

Part II

SURVIVE

Relieving Stress

1

Having a Vision

This first strategy can minimize the greatest amount of stress and conflict. Many engaged couples fail to articulate their vision for their wedding day, possibly without even realizing it. This approach will eliminate many conflicts before they arise.

The couple and their parents should have a meeting to talk about the couple's vision for the big day. This helps the parents learn *what* the couple wants and *how best they can help* them make it happen, and the couple understand what's important to the parents. Topics to discuss might include:

- when the wedding will happen—setting on a date
- the marriage ceremony—a nuptial Mass versus a nuptial ceremony
- ideas for guest activities between the wedding (for church weddings) and reception
- what kind of reception is desired (formal, casual, or something different?)
- what type of venue is desired and where will it be (location?)
- the size of the guest list (large vs. small)
- what kind of music (live band, DJ, or something else?)

- flowers and other decorations, making sure to include flowers for the church
- whether to use a photographer or videographer
- whether to invite children under a certain age
- the financial roles of parents and the couple

The more the couple and parents know of one another's viewpoints, the smoother the entire process will be. For example, it is important for parents to know whether the couple wants a small, formal, one-hundred-guest reception in a traditional catering hall two years from now or a two-hundred-guest wedding in a park in a few months.

After this initial meeting, we suggest that all the parents—including exes and stepparents—have a second meeting to discuss what they've learned. The objective is for all parents to agree that, as a group, they want to help the couple in any way possible to make the big day special, and what each parent can do toward this goal.

One idea is to write a brief vision for the couple for their wedding day. The parents should agree to *offer* the couple help in several areas based on personal experiences, expertise, financial capability, and contacts:

- For financial assistance, see chapter 22, "Who Pays for What?"
- For the review of contracts with vendors, see chapter 27, "Negotiations and Contracts."
- For evaluating vendors, see chapters 1 to 8.

For example, if one of the parents is an attorney, he or she can offer to review vendor contracts. If the parents know a DJ, they can provide the contact information. The key is to *offer* the couple help and advice and provide suggestions—but also listen to what the couple wants. These meetings can dramatically reduce the stress and angst for the entire wedding-planning process.

REFLECTION

Many couples wish that they had created a vision statement early in the planning process so that everyone clearly understood their desires from the beginning.

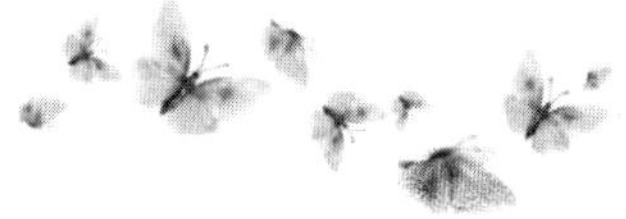

2

Being Obsessed with Perfection

Sometimes a TV sitcom like *Last Man Standing* can teach us a great lesson, and in this case it addresses one that plagues so many brides and grooms: *perfection*. They drive themselves, and those around them, crazy with the desire to make everything perfect.

In one episode of this series, the bride-to-be became a "bridezilla," wanting every single detail, no matter how small, to be perfect. The groom went along because he wanted her to be happy. His only request was that he wanted to wear white high-top sneakers to the wedding.

This, of course, caused a major argument until he told his fiancée *why* he wanted to wear them. When he had gone for an interview for his current job, he borrowed a suit but forgot to borrow shoes. His only shoes were white high-top sneakers, so he went to the interview in a suit and sneakers. At the interview, the owner of the establishment looked at his shoes and said, "kid, you're one of a kind, I want you on my team." And it was through this job that he met his bride.

For him, the sneakers were the reason he found happiness with the woman of his dreams. Once the bride heard the story, she cried and realized that there is no such thing as a perfect wedding, and what really matters is that the two people getting married are surrounded by family and friends who love them. Of course he wore the sneakers, and it was a "perfect" ceremony.

So, like the bride in the story, if you try too hard to reach perfection, you might very well miss those special "moments." The lesson here is to enjoy every minute of your wedding: talk to those who love you; kick off your shoes and dance up a storm like no one's watching. Savor the food; drink the drinks. Go off your pre-wedding diet. Hug everyone. Spend a little quality time with people who have come a long way to celebrate with you.

Above all, let love rule the day and don't fret over any problems. Now, *that's* the true definition of perfection.

To paraphrase a famous saying, "Planning a wedding is a journey, so enjoy the ride."

REFLECTION

To avoid getting consumed by the details, some couples take "timeouts," during which they don't talk about the stress and issues to clear their minds and stop the constant pursuit of perfection. They seek to minimize confrontation with their family and friends by responding positively to suggestions or acting graciously when demands are made.

SCRIPTURE

> He said to his disciples, "Therefore I tell you, do not worry about your life, what you will eat, or about your body, what you will wear. For life is more than food, and the body more than clothing." (Luke 12:22–23)

Perhaps this was Jesus's way of saying, "Don't sweat the small things or the big things and enjoy the journey. Hand your problems over to God, who will provide for you."

3

"It's Our Wedding" versus "It's Our Money"

No, this is not *Monday Night Football* with the helmets of the two opposing teams banging into each other and exploding. But this is about a conflict that's been going on for decades, if not centuries—the wants and needs of the couple versus the wants and needs of the parents, who are paying for some, most, or even all of the wedding.

Some couples feel that, *because it's their day*, they get to call all the shots.

Some parents feel that, *because it's their money*, they get to call all the shots.

Of course, the right answer is somewhere in between, and the goal is to get everyone on the same page. The bottom line is that money can buy material things at a wedding but *not* most intangible things. Yes, money buys the food, music, and flowers. But money should never buy "rights"—like the right to invite certain people or the right to determine who makes a toast.

Since this issue is at the core of most—if not all—family conflicts in planning a wedding, we've noted what people have said. The consensus:

- This really is the couple's day. Make no mistake about that. But this doesn't mean the couple should ignore requests from parents and other family members.
- Yes, the parents may be paying, but holding the payment over the heads of the couple is not fair or acceptable.
- A Zola (wedding platform) survey indicates that brides and grooms put much of the blame for their wedding-planning stress on their parents and future in-laws. This must change.
- When couples and parents take the time and effort to listen to and understand one another and reach a compromise, the "us versus them" approach becomes a nonissue. Suddenly, the couple and parents discover the joy of compromise.

For example, after one couple had decided on a specific date for their wedding, they were reminded by a parent that the chosen date was an important religious holiday and that many people might not be able to attend. Rather than stick to their date, the couple decided to change it, showing that they were flexible and aware of the needs of others.

Similarly, a different couple who wanted a small wedding reception noted that, because they couldn't invite everyone that they and the parents wanted to, they asked everyone involved to make an equal number of cuts to the guest list to be fair to all. How could anyone argue with that logic?

Another issue to address up front is the potential cost for guests to attend and how your choices can play a role in their decisions.

REFLECTION

Most couples recognize that while this is *their* day, it is also very important to their parents. They express the importance of finding the right balance between their desires and the requests of their parents. In most cases, finding this balance is a good formula.

4

The Role of the Parents

While parents look forward to the day their child gets married, they may not necessarily look forward to giving up their role as the primary source of information, advice, and guidance. It's time to recognize that your child's partner is now top dog.

From our experience, discussions, and research, it's important for parents to embrace the idea that the couple's most important duty is to each other, as they will be making decisions together every day of their lives. While they are two different people, they have become partners in all aspects. After all, that's the meaning of the vows they make to each other.

It's also likely that this move away from the parents and toward each other started long before the couple announced their engagement. It's part of the process of becoming a new nuclear family.

Parents who don't accept this and try to remain central in their child's life will almost always encounter problems.

This change doesn't mean that parents' opinions and advice should not be heard. Far from it. What it does mean is that the couple and all parents involved should work together for a healthy, productive, and enjoyable partnership.

Parents may recall when they were newly engaged and how they moved from relying on their parents for advice to becoming an independent couple. While times have changed, this dynamic really hasn't.

Couples may consider the wise guidance parents have provided them from birth and continue to seek their guidance as part of their decision-making process.

REFLECTION

Many couples express the desire for their parents to step back and let them make their own decisions, even if they may not be the best ones. They feel that they can learn from their own mistakes.

They understand how difficult it is for their parents to let go in planning such a large event with so many moving parts. They emphasize the need for space and want reassurance that, in the end, if they don't take some advice, their parents will still fully support them.

SCRIPTURE

> Do to others as you would have them do to you. (Luke 6:31)

When discussing any issue, place yourself in the other person's shoes. This adds perspective to both sides.

5

In-Law Harmony

Despite all the jokes, harmony with one's in-laws is indeed possible. And it is true what they say to couples, "You're marrying your in-laws as well as each other."

We've heard stories from the good to the bad and the ugly when it comes to in-law relationships. But we also know that with some effort, the likelihood of in-law harmony increases dramatically.

With new people in the couple's life—parents of the bride or groom, siblings, perhaps an ex, a stepfamily, or a birth family—there's a good deal to process. But what we've experienced and heard from countless couples and parents is the value of making the in-law relationships work.

All stakeholders—the couple and all family members—should make a pact to work at integrating everyone in an enjoyable way. Maybe the couple invites the parents for a brunch, or the bride's parents invite everyone for a picnic, or the groom's parents get together with the bride's parents (without the couple) to get to know one another.

That's ideal, but what happens when it doesn't go smoothly? Everyone should remember that the couple is now a team and that each has the other's back. That must be nonnegotiable for the marriage to work. Remember that the parents have the best interests of the couple at heart, and their opinions and suggestions deserve to be heard.

When the feelings are positive, issues like the following can be more easily resolved:

- In order to make sure the bride's overbearing mother does not push her into ordering flowers she doesn't want, the groom accompanies them to the florist.
- With one small family and one large family, a discussion occurs about the size of the wedding. Together, everyone agrees to a small ceremony the night before and a larger reception on the day of the wedding. Everyone's needs are met.
- Based on input from parents and siblings, the bride and groom award honors during the ceremony (or reception) to some people they hadn't considered beforehand.

Now, suppose the couple encounter a difficult issue that can't be resolved. In such cases, it may be time to talk to your priest, deacon, trusted lay minister, or mentor couple if you are working with one. It may even be worth having a conversation with a therapist to get feedback. In addition, consider utilizing a wedding planner as a buffer between families who are in conflict.

Everyone should vocalize such sentiments as "There's nothing more important than harmonious family relationships, and we commit to doing everything possible to have one with you."

REFLECTION

Some couples decide what is important and then agree to tell parents their decision. They also believe that they need to be strong together for this to work. One couple voices their desire to compromise, but there are times when they have to take a stand against an unreasonable demand. Finally, one couple decides to pay for the wedding to avoid a controlling mother's interference.

THE LIGHTER SIDE OF IN-LAW RELATIONSHIPS

There are thousands of medical diagnosis codes, those letters and numbers that identify specific illnesses. Google code Z63.1 and you'll see that it relates to "problems in relationship with in-laws." Really, it's a thing—no kidding.

Therefore, if the happy couple and parents follow our recommendations for communication, collaboration, and compromise, we doubt the diagnosis code Z63.1 will be in your future!

6

Truth and Consequences

From the time a couple contemplates their engagement, it is possible that parents and others may see, hear, or read something that raises serious questions about the viability of the pending marriage. The good news for couples preparing for marriage in the Catholic Church is that the primary goal of marriage preparation is to ensure that the couple is truly compatible and able (i.e., has the capacity) for a lifelong, healthy, and successful marriage.

It is the duty of the priest or deacon to make sure, to the best of his ability, that nothing stands in the way of a permanent, faithful, lifegiving, valid Catholic marriage. In other words, if an issue surfaces during the marriage preparation process that is serious enough to affect the capacity or free consent of the couple to contract a Catholic marriage, the priest or deacon will develop a practical, pastoral plan to deal with the issue.

Depending on the issue, the couple may be referred for psychological, medical, or theological evaluation, with an action plan for moving forward. Sometimes, this means delaying the marriage to work on the issue, *or* it may mean that the priest or deacon cannot, in good conscience, move forward with the marriage.

When parents, siblings, co-workers, or friends of the couple become aware of a serious situation that has not been revealed in the marriage-preparation sessions, they can ask to meet with the pastor of the parish where the marriage will take place even if they are not Catholic. The pastor is trained to deal with such situations.

7

Out of Sight, Out of Mind

Physical distance between the couple and parents can create stress. It's very easy to "forget" about working with those who live far away, but doing so can easily lead to conflict and resentment. Consider these examples:

- The couple lives in the New York City area, as does one set of parents. The other parents live in Florida. It's easy for the couple to get together to plan with the parents that live close by but virtually impossible to meet as frequently with the ones living in Florida.
- The couple lives in Ohio, one set of parents lives in Virginia, and the other set lives in California. Unless money is no object, meeting even once during the wedding-planning process can be problematic.
- All three couples live within an hour drive of one another, which makes it much easier to meet.

No one wants to feel left out. Generally, everyone wants to contribute and play a role. No one wants to be the victim of "out of sight, out of mind." Fortunately, today it's easy to have remote meetings via Zoom, FaceTime, or Skype. It's not the same thing as meeting face-to-face, but they are very good alternatives.

From the get-go, the couple and parents should agree to have regular meetings, either in person or virtually. Making time for inclusive planning helps establish warm relationships between the couple and both sets of parents.

REFLECTION

Some couples note that it is very important to schedule video call meetings to make sure everyone feels included and that an "out of sight, out of mind" situation doesn't happen.

8

It's All about Fairness

When it comes to relationships, triangles are almost always tricky. When it comes to wedding planning, the couple and the two sets of parents form a triangle that is either equilateral or not. At the core of the optimal wedding triangle is *fairness.*

At times, it may be easy for the couple to favor one set of parents over the other, whether intentionally or not. The triangle can become unbalanced when one set of parents is treated better than the other.

Fairness in this context means that all stakeholders—the couple and both sets of parents—feel they are being treated fairly and that no one feels cheated:

- Unless there's a good reason—bigger family, more friends and business contacts—one set of parents gets to invite more people than the other—that's not fair.
- One set of parents gets more wedding day honors than the other, perhaps due to the size of the family. Again, not fair unless there's a good reason.
- All parents are listed in the program—that's fair.
- Each parent gets a dance—that's fair.
- Songs requested by one set of parents are played but those requested by the other are not, unless discussed beforehand—that may not be fair, depending on the tunes.

Most importantly, fairness needs to travel back and forth in four directions (and more when including blended families):

- between the couple and her parents
- between the couple and his parents
- between the bride and groom
- between both sets of parents

To be effective, fairness should supersede money. If her parents are paying for the entire wedding or contributing more to it, his parents should still be treated fairly, both by her parents and by the couple. The amount of financial support should not influence decisions.

Throughout the planning process, you never want to hear "We're not being treated fairly," because that sets a bad precedent for now and later.

In terms of responding to most requests by family and friends, a good response is "That's a great idea. I will talk with my fiancé(e) and see how best to incorporate it. I'd love to find ways for all our wishes, including yours, to be realized" (skylarkclinic.ca.).

REFLECTION

Some couples note that what goes along with fairness is how you react to adversity. They point out that it is easy to get defensive and react immediately to what others say, but in retrospect it is not always the best response. They comment that it would have been better to tell the other person(s), "Let us think about that," and then discuss choices with their partners and tackle the issue once the couple is on the same page.

9

The Importance of Clear Messages

How often have you heard a politician say "Let me be clear" and what follows is misleading murkiness? All the time, right? Well, planning a wedding must be the opposite to ensure that everyone involved is on the same page. Statements can be interpreted in many ways, which is why clear messages are so important.

We've heard numerous times that both couples and parents *thought* they knew what was supposed to happen or what they were supposed to do but the reality was often different.

And the culprit? The couples and parents were not clear about what they agreed upon regarding the specific issue. It's easy to fall into this trap, as family discussions can be fun but change course quickly. Furthermore, people sometimes "hear what they want to hear," and that must also be taken into consideration.

What's needed is an all-pro quarterback (QB) who keeps everyone focused during meetings about the wedding. It could be the bride, groom, or another designated person who takes notes, keeps discussions on track, and emails a summary afterward. It could also be the wedding planner if you have hired one for the wedding.

In addition to the QB, no one should assume anything, because you know what happens when someone does. If there's a question, no matter how small, about any decision, it needs to be voiced and answered. The last thing you want is for someone, months down the road, to say, "Well, I thought it was going to be an open bar," and someone else says, "I remember talking about beer, wine, and soft drinks only."

For every topic and decision, a clear message, such as "We want to have our wedding in the fall" or "We are flexible in terms of the day of the week and even time of the day" is important.

Clear statements such as "Mom and Dad, it would be a big help if you could review all the contracts" or "Sis, can you help me organize a database of email addresses?" leave little room for error.

To complete the process, the parent, sibling, or person involved should repeat their understanding of what's been asked so that nothing is lost in the translation.

Couples must keep in mind that parents and siblings want to be involved, and likewise, parents and siblings must recognize that involvement doesn't mean diverging from what the couple has indicated they want. Parents, if you can't do what the couple wants, don't accept the assignment but say "That's not good for me" and request a different one.

When it comes to money, clarity is essential. If parents are contributing and would like input on how the money is spent, then the couple and parents need to talk about the budget to clarify who is paying for what expenses.

REFLECTION

We have often heard about the lack of clarity, like one groom, for example, who said that there was not enough communication at the outset about who does what and who pays for what. Everyone can get caught up in the moment and make vague "promises" that later cause confusion.

10

Flexibility Is a Virtue

Like a gymnast whose body is limber and flexible, couples and parents need to have flexible minds when it comes to wedding planning. Instead of fighting change, you must embrace it.

From minor details to major decisions, there will be many times where being flexible leads to the best possible decision. Consider the following examples:

- The couple has their heart set on a wedding in the city. But when they and the parents paying for it see the price tag, they understand the need to be *flexible* and consider a suburban setting at a much lower cost.
- The bride is certain about the dress she wants, but when she sees others that are better suited for her, she becomes *flexible* in considering a dress other than her first choice.
- When an adopted bride's mother, who has been the primary female role model in her daughter's life, understands that she wants her biological mother to share in the day, she demonstrates her *flexibility* by encouraging an invitation (see chapter 16, "A Place for Birth Families?").

- When the bride realizes that it doesn't make sense for all her bridesmaids to have the same dress, she becomes *flexible* by asking that each bridesmaid choose her own style, but all within the same color palette.
- While the groom wants a destination bachelor party, he becomes *flexible* because some of his groomsmen can't afford to fly to a tropical island.

Flexibility is not about settling for something less. It's about making changes that result in something more.

Couples and parents often use the term "perfect wedding" (see chapter 2, "Being Obsessed with Perfection") as they want every detail to be perfect. However, as we all know, life doesn't work this way. And what's perfect for one person may not always be perfect for everyone.

When the shuttle from the church to the venue is delayed, moving the reception back a half hour is the prudent thing to do, despite it being the less-than-perfect option. When the second bartender gets sick and the venue can't find another one, some guests may have to wait longer than usual for their drinks. No need to stress, for there's nothing that can be done in this situation.

Remember, always make lemonade out of lemons, and the big day will be fabulous even if it's not perfect.

One father waxed philosophically about the weddings in his family, noting that "the wedding is over in one day. It's the rest of everyone's lives that are important." He also talked about how the couple felt about the day and how it was more important than how he felt. Family is just too darn important to let one-day issues ruin things. He recalled how one relative had not spoken to his daughter for thirty years due to a wedding flare-up. His summation: step back and smell the roses.

REFLECTION

One couple dealt with the issue of what songs to play by noting everyone's request and asking the DJ to play each of them throughout the party. The couple's favorites comprised the lion's share, but they were pleased that many guests got to hear one requested song. Another couple had the DJ announce some of the requests, like, "This one's for you, mother and father of the bride!"

11

Getting on the Same Page

It's time for a pop quiz. Which approach do you think would be most effective?

- The couple plans the entire wedding and informs the parents, "All you have to do is show up on the big day."
- The couple and parents, and maybe even a few others, work together as a team from day one, constantly communicating to ensure the best possible wedding and have a stress-free planning process.

While the first approach can work in certain circumstances, most families favor the second approach, which will almost always work and greatly reduce stress. While many couples involve their parents, assign tasks, and seek guidance, what's missing from many of these "partnerships" is constant communication. With hundreds of details, it's easy for things to fall through the cracks, especially when there are at least six people involved.

A great way to keep everything organized and running smoothly is for the couple to host weekly meetings by phone or virtually or send updates by email or text. We've met couples who have formalized this approach by scheduling a video call every Friday morning. Others send out a weekly email update.

There's no right approach to communicate these updates except that they need to be clear and regular. Here are three additional good reasons to be conscientious about your communications:

- Parents feel connected to the couple's plans and comfortable about making important contributions.
- In addition to their friends and the internet, couples have four or more additional people off whom to bounce ideas—people who have some experience and expertise.
- Couples and parents develop the ability to work together harmoniously, which is extremely valuable for the future.

It's also a great approach when the couple and one or more of the parents don't live close to one another and cannot attend in-person meetings. If the couple and their parents, for example, live in three different states, planning can be more of a challenge than if they lived within twenty minutes of one another (see chapter 7, "Out of Sight, Out of Mind"). Getting on the same page through weekly communication is the way to go.

REFLECTION

Most couples feel that frequent and clear communication is a lifesaver in their planning process. With so many tasks to juggle, they appreciate it when their helpers keep them posted about their specific tasks and vice versa. Couples that don't have a lot of communication, however, note that, if they had to do it again, they would put more emphasis on keeping in touch and making sure everyone was on the same page.

SCRIPTURE

> With all humility and gentleness, with patience, bearing with one another through love. (Ephesians 4:2)

Adhering to this passage, combined with compromise, communication, and collaboration, makes for a wonderful marriage and life.

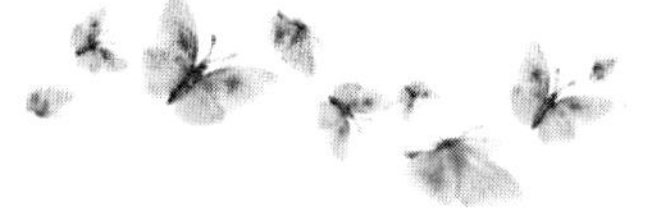

12

Understanding Priorities

"We're getting married. Let's go dress shopping today." Wow! Let's take a step back and make sure everyone is on the same page in terms of priorities in planning the wedding. It's easy to understand that in the excitement, the couple wants to do all the fun stuff first: looking at venues, dresses, bands, and so on; however, there's not much excitement about creating a budget, looking at wedding insurance, or thinking about a shuttle service.

Parents, especially those who have assisted in planning weddings with other children or know the ins and outs from friends, can guide and advise the couple and help them understand the order of priorities.

The top priorities that everyone should consider are:

- the couple's vision for the wedding (see chapter 1, "Having a Vision")
- the budget for all components of the wedding
- an approximate date for the wedding
- the potential number of guests to be invited

The objective in setting good priorities is to avoid wasting time. Why look at venues until you know how many people will attend and when it will be held? Why run around listening to bands if live music is not financially possible?

And keep in mind that some things need a longer lead time than others.

The couple and parents should break the wedding-planning timeline into chunks of time and address specific tasks and decisions within each chunk.

There are plenty of wedding-planning timelines, tools, and apps that can be found online. Pick one you like and make sure everyone involved has access to it.

The best thing parents can do is explain *why* certain tasks and decisions should be made before others. Since the couple probably has not been through this process before, they can draw upon the experience of their parents so that everything gets done on time.

Of course, getting the priorities straight reduces stress and conflicts.

But wait. There are three other priorities that everyone must embrace from day one to the wedding day:

- This is a happy occasion. Find the fun in planning each event and activity.
- Look for the silver lining in the disagreements—you'll always find one.
- Celebrate special moments as you explore options for the special day.

REFLECTION

As you would expect, nearly all the couples we spoke with noted that they were super excited and focused on looking at venues, dresses, and the "fun stuff," but they realized the budget was where they needed to start so they wouldn't waste time looking at options that were too expensive. Many said that their parents were very helpful in keeping them focused so they could make good decisions early on.

13

Whom to Invite

Creating the guest list can either be simple and easy or a great source of angst for everyone involved. Start with the immediate families—bride, groom, and parents—and then mix in, if necessary, former spouses, stepfamily members, siblings, birth parents, significant others, and children. You can see that this can get very complicated, especially if people don't get along or if you want a small wedding but have more people than you may want to invite.

Chapter 1, "Having a Vision," provides helpful material for dealing with this potentially thorny issue. The first thing that the couple needs to discuss with the parents is the total number of guests, and the approximate number of guests in each of the following groups:

- the bride's family and the groom's family
- friends of the couple
- friends of the parents
- any exes, significant others, "plus ones," or stepfamily members
- children under eighteen if they are to be invited

The couple and parents should each make a wish list of whom they want to invite. Code each one with *must* invite or *would like* to invite but not necessary. Based on location and other issues, indicate which invitees in the lists are not likely to attend if invited.

The parents should count the number of guests likely to attend and let the couple know how many are in each group—*must* invite or *would like* to invite. If the total of all lists is at or under the total number of guests, then a lot of pain has been avoided. When creating the lists, it's a good idea to put a percentage figure next to each invite relating to the probability that they will attend. Example: Aunt Bee and Uncle Dee, who live 1,500 miles away—25 percent. This will help you visualize how many people are likely to attend. But if there are too many guests, there are two options:

- The parents can start pruning their list so that it's fair and equitable.
- Parents who go over their guest allotment might offer to pay for extra guests if the venue has space and the couple agrees.

While the wedding day is special for the happy couple and is basically *their* day, they should realize that it is also special for the proud parents. Parents long to share this special day with family and close friends, and even people from work. Understanding this will help the couple see their parents' perspective.

Like other wedding-planning situations, fair, open, and honest communication combined with everyone's willingness to compromise will help resolve this issue.

REFLECTION

We have often heard that couples and parents have their own set of criteria about whom to invite. When considering whom to invite, couples ask questions like "Do you have a personal or family connection with this person?" or "Will they make the wedding more fun?" Today, couples are concerned, given the high cost of weddings, about inviting every Tom, Dick, and Harry at the expense of those with whom they have a relationship. In the TV series *Jane the Virgin*, the title character Jane states, "If we haven't met them, they can't come. Period!" Many couples, however, say that they don't want to deprive their parents of special people in their lives.

14

What about the Children?

One of the most emotionally charged issues that can cause long-term negative resentments and problems is whether to invite children to the ceremony and reception. We know of situations where intense feelings of resentment about uninvited children remain years after the wedding.

It's easy to understand why couples and even their parents may choose not to invite children, especially young children, to the wedding. They can be noisy and unruly, and they draw attention away from the bride and groom.

Not inviting children, however, can really upset some people, especially siblings, grandparents, and close friends.

Even if it's decided, for example, that there will be "no kids under eighteen," people will lobby for exceptions. Maybe the bride is very close to an eight-year-old niece, or the groom has a disabled teenage friend. Both very reasonable reasons for an exception, but both run the risk of prompting wedding-day comments like "Well, you invited Maria, but why not my son?"

One option is to explain who will be invited and why, and what exceptions will be made in advance of the day. There's still the risk that people will be upset.

So, here's one possible solution: all children may attend the ceremony, but it's incumbent upon the parents to keep them well-behaved during that time.

While the adults attend the reception, the children gather in a different room with their own party. Their food is substantially cheaper (chicken fingers and hot dogs are traditional), and a few hired chaperones can supervise. Most venues have a separate room for this purpose, and in the grand scheme of things it should not add much cost.

The bride and groom can even stop in to the "kids' party" for a few minutes to say hi.

This solution could easily remove all possible resentments and grudges.

REFLECTION

Some couples note that they know from the start that they do not want children at the reception. Some feel the opposite, especially when children have been present at prior weddings and family get-togethers. Many couples find the "ceremony only" option with a separate "kiddie reception" a great compromise and recognize the need to include children to avoid years of resentment.

SCRIPTURE

> Above all, maintain constant love for one another,
> for love covers a multitude of sins. (1 Peter 4:8)

Love also conquers unreasonable demands and difficult personalities.

15

Making Demands

The last thing anyone needs is for a war to break out in the middle of the planning process. As the song goes, "War, what is it good for? Absolutely nothing."

Let's consider one scenario: the bride's parents experienced a bitter divorce and have not been speaking to each other for years. The bride *is* close to both. The groom is also on good terms with both parents.

By one parent making a blanket statement or demand that if the other is going to attend, then he or she will not, that parent is deliberately putting the couple between a rock and a hard place, forcing them to choose one over the other. Now is the time for parents, exes, stepparents, and others intimately involved to get on the same page and resolve any issues to do with the wedding, thereby setting a precedent for the future. The exes don't have to get along every other day of the year—that's their business. But on "family days," exes need to chill out and play nice for the children and grandchildren.

While the parents in the above example may seem to be miles apart, the couple first needs to decide what they want, and if they want both at the wedding, they must devise a plan to get everyone on board.

The plan might be as simple as doing everything possible to keep the warring parents away from each other, without having to play the role of monitor on the big day. Here's how that might work:

- seating them at different tables
- having them walk down the aisle separately
- having them make separate toasts, speeches, or readings
- thanking them publicly for the positive role they have played
- giving them different assignments to help with the planning
- asking them to do different nonconflicting tasks for or during the reception

While the conversation will likely be uncomfortable, the couple should not put it off. The sooner it's resolved, the better.

If the divorced parents continue to be entrenched in their position about the other being invited or attending, the couple has no choice but to try a "tough love" approach such as the following:

> Mom, Dad, we love you both, and we want you both at our wedding. Since you cannot stop bickering, we have no choice but to flip a coin. Do you really want everyone asking where the parent is that lost the coin toss?

Whatever approach you take, choose one that you feel comfortable with and may yield the best results.

Finally, give the parents time to think about it. Maybe they'll come to an agreement on their own, and the problem will resolve itself.

REFLECTION

One couple took a hardline approach to this issue, saying to her parents, "We can't have two weddings, one for each of you. If you can't figure this out without causing more conflict, then I don't want either of you there."

16

A Place for Birth Families?

If the bride or groom is adopted, then embracing the birth family can be extremely emotional. Of course, much depends on the circumstances surrounding the adoption, the childhood of the adopted person, and if any relationship has been fostered between the birth mother/father and the adoptive family.

Very simply, the person has two moms: the one that gave the child life and the one that raised and nurtured the child.

The most important lesson we have heard repeatedly is that both relationships are precious, and each has its own special attachments.

One mom of an adopted daughter stated that, since the birth parents had allowed her and her husband to raise and love their child, they had no problem when the daughter asked them if her birth parents could be invited to the wedding.

The primary conflict that can occur with inviting birth families is when the parent or parents who raised the adopted child do not want to share the moment with the birth parent(s). This can be a source of great anxiety.

Parents of adoptive children may want to think about how their child will feel if they object to inviting the birth family.

Both the adoptive and birth parents should try to remember that each relationship is special, and each relationship should be cherished by the child for who that person is in his or her life. Depending on the age of the adopted child when he or she marries, the role of the adoptive parents shouldn't be diminished by the presence of the birth family.

As with every other potential issue in this book, the adoptive parents and their engaged child need to have an open and honest conversation. Each side needs to hear the other's wishes and desires and work together to find common ground.

Having attended a few weddings where the birth family was present, I have noticed that they generally seem to have a great time without experiencing any acrimony.

REFLECTION

Couples usually appreciate their parents giving them permission to make the decision about inviting a birth family with their blessings. We also noted that there is greater benefit in raising and discussing potential issues as early as possible, sometimes even before the engagement is announced.

SCRIPTURE

> With all humility and gentleness, with patience, bearing with one another in love, making every effort to maintain the unity of the Spirit in the bond of peace. (Ephesians 4:2–3)

When we exhibit characteristics of humility, gentleness, patience, and love toward others as we plan the wedding, we can help maintain a sense of peace throughout the process.

17

What about Extended Families?

In situations where there are large families and/or stepfamilies, it can be very easy to exceed budget. And what happens if the groom wants a large wedding but the bride envisions a small, intimate one?

If this sounds like your situation, it will be helpful for you to discuss this early in the process; it can be a very emotional issue that shouldn't go unresolved.

This story is about a bride who wanted a small, intimate church wedding. It's also about a groom who comes from an extended family—one where cousins are more like brothers and sisters and celebrating together is a family tradition—and wanted a large wedding.

Now, this couple agreed on the perfect compromise.

The night before the wedding reception, they had an intimate religious ceremony with their nuclear families followed by a dinner for family and close friends.

The wedding reception the following day was the big celebration, where all of the extended family was invited to keep the family tradition intact.

But suppose this couple couldn't agree on what to do. What next?

Parents may intervene to help the couple think about the many relationships that are at stake, and whether it is worth alienating close relatives that have been in the groom's life for decades. They can also talk about the importance of ensuring that the bride's dream wedding happens.

Another point parents can make is that, in life, you don't always get everything you want, and the art of compromise will serve them well. Luckily, this couple didn't need to be steered in that direction since they compromised right away.

REFLECTION

In our experience, many couples know that budget constraints are a determining factor in the number of guests to be invited and make a list of those people they have to invite. They ask the parents to do the same. This helps everyone focus on whom to invite (see chapter 13).

In some cases, couples and parents agree that invitees not on the "must have" lists would be paid for by the parents. During the COVID-19 pandemic, for example, some couples held their small Catholic wedding on their original date, then a larger reception later.

18

People You Can't Invite

For whatever reason, there are usually some people you cannot invite. In most cases, the bride and groom decide on a maximum number, forcing them to exclude some people. But there are things you can do to turn a disappointing and even hurtful situation into a positive one.

SOFTEN THE BLOW

What you say when delivering the bad news can make up, to some extent, for delivering the "sorry, you can't come" message. In this situation, the following approach makes good sense:

> I'm having a real hard time with something that I want to discuss with you. I really want you and your spouse at the wedding, but I'm running into a venue capacity and cost roadblock. Between two families, all the couple's friends, extended families, special friends, and more, we're not going to be able to invite everyone we want. So, while we can't invite you to the reception, it would mean a great deal to us if you could attend the wedding at the church.

DURING THE WEDDING

See if you can arrange to livestream the reception speeches. If so, ask the bride and groom to say a few words directly to the group viewing the wedding remotely.

AFTER THE WEDDING

Throw a post-wedding party for the uninvited and show a video of the ceremony. It would be the next best thing to being there and much less than the cost per plate had they been invited in the first place. Consider asking the now-married couple to attend, if possible.

While the uninvited will likely understand because limitations are commonplace, showing that you really care and are going out of your way to "make up" for it shows how much you value these relationships. One mom of four talked about the importance of calling, not emailing or texting, people who can't be invited and explaining why, to minimize hurt feelings. A simple phone call goes a long way.

REFLECTION

One couple celebrated their wedding in another country, and their grandparents could not make the trip, so the couple streamed the ceremony and parts of the reception to them and others who could not be there. They also paid tribute to the mother of the bride who had recently passed away by using a picture of the bride's mom and attaching a locket with a picture of her mom to the bouquet.

SCRIPTURE

> Little children, let us love, not in word or speech, but in truth and action. (1 John 3:18)

It is best for everyone involved when you are open and honest when planning the wedding.

19

Reducing Stress through Prayer

This suggestion for relieving stress may seem a little different from the others. We're not offering suggestions on how someone else can help you in the wedding-planning process. We're not offering advice on how to select a venue or florist.

What we are suggesting is that you turn your worries, concerns, and joys over to God by embracing prayer during this time. Why? Prayer gives hope, the ultimate stress reliever. We know that more than half of Americans pray each day, as do 20 percent of people not even affiliated with a religion. Many doctors admit that it's the best thing you can do for your mind and body.

Prayer is simply a conversation with God, during which we ask for guidance, tell God our problems, and listen to what God is telling us. You don't have to go to church to pray. You can pray at home, while driving, or even while waiting in line at the supermarket. That's what's so great—God is always there to listen to us.

You don't have to recite a specific prayer; you can put your thoughts into your own words. They can be as simple as "Jesus give me the strength today to handle whatever comes" or "Lord, guide me in my decisions today." And pray as often as you want; there are no limits. You can even create a prayer to get you through the wedding-planning process.

Through prayer you can offer praise and worship to God, thanksgiving for your many blessings, especially for one another and our families, or request to be the best person you can be. Most of all, prayer should be a way to offer thanks for the many gifts and guidance God is giving you.

Prayer can also be more formal. There are many prayers that can be found on the internet. Consider, for example, this one:

> I pray that the peace of Christ rules in my family's hearts (Colossians 3:15). Show us how to be united and to live in harmony with one another and be thankful for one another. In Jesus's name, Amen.

You can also talk to a priest, minister, pastor, premarital counselor, or any clergy about praying to reduce stress over the issues you are facing. Doing so may help you resolve specific situations.

REFLECTION

Since 2004, Peg has worked with hundreds of Catholic and many interfaith couples during the planning process for their weddings, and without a doubt, those who prayed regularly dealt with stress and conflict most effectively.

20

Sibling Rivalries

Putting relationships with the parents aside, there is another group—siblings—that can cause potential stress. And the more siblings the couple has, the more complicated it can be. The questions the couple will encounter include:

- Should all siblings be invited to the wedding?
- Should all who attend be in the wedding party?
- Is it wrong to choose a best friend instead of a brother to be best man?
- Is it wrong to choose a best friend instead of a sister for a bridesmaid, maid/matron of honor?
- What should I do about stepsiblings, especially if we're not close?
- Which of my two sisters should be maid of honor?
- How will my brother feel if I don't choose him as my best man?

Brides and grooms we've spoken with about this issue talk about the relationship with their siblings versus the relationship with their friends. Perhaps the answer starts with making a list of all potential honors:

- maid/matron of honor, best man
- bridesmaids, groomsmen

- readers (first or second reading, psalm, or petitions)
- offertory gift bearers, flower girl, ring bearer
- speakers and toast makers at the reception
- people who sing or play an instrument at weddings or receptions
- people reading a poem or inspirational quote or saying a prayer or blessing at the reception

Make a list of all siblings and others whom you want to receive an honor. Once you have all the names, match up parents, friends, and siblings to the various honors. Even if you give an honor to *every* sibling, spreading them out over a four- or five-hour period in both the ceremony and reception will not slow things down.

The bottom line is that no one likes to be left out, and everyone will likely be fine with one role or another. Hopefully a sibling that you're not that close to will understand not being chosen as best man or bridesmaid or matron of honor but will be happy to participate in some other way.

This is also a great opportunity to mend fences. If you've been at odds with a sibling, say, "My wedding is a new chapter in my life, I want you in it and hopefully we can jump-start our relationship. Let's make amends and move forward... sound good?" It's also an opportunity to welcome siblings from your future spouse's side and even stepsiblings, showing them how wonderful it is that these two families are coming together.

REFLECTION

One bride who had a difficult relationship with her sister was torn about having her in the wedding party. Soon after being engaged, she made plans to meet with her sister and discuss their differences. The bride included her sister in some of the planning and, based on how the meeting went, asked her to be a bridesmaid. The bride recalled that taking that first step was one of the best decisions she ever made.

21

Embracing New Relationships

Three types of relationships can occur when the couple's families "marry each other":

1. A contentious, mistrustful, and argumentative relationship,
2. A harmonious, healthy, and happy relationship, or
3. Somewhere between these extremes.

Clearly there's no choice. Choosing the middle option is obvious. The last one can work also, but it's not as desirable as the middle option.

So, how do you ensure that there's no subtle or overt hostility when two new families come together through an engagement?

The simple answer is that it's like any relationship: you work at it.

Begin with a new mindset. Instead of "my family" and "your family," consider saying "our family." Think of a circle with the couple in the middle and both families, including any extended family members, circling them and embracing them with love.

It's a great idea for the couple or one of the parents to invite everyone to a fun get-together shortly after the marriage is announced. One mom remembered how a boat trip quickly brought the families together where they had all afternoon and into the evening to get to know one another.

Why is doing fun things like this so important?

Once families get to know one another and hopefully find they enjoy spending time together, they are less likely to argue and be unwilling to compromise. In many cases the parents will realize how much they have in common, and that can only lead to good things. If that is not the case, sharing a fun-filled experience is a good basis for cooperation.

Even if they don't become "best buds," they will be friendly at family gatherings, and that is much better than the alternative.

REFLECTION

One couple noted that getting the families together well before the wedding was so important, and that they made sure that the time was for something fun and not for wedding planning. In these situations, families became comfortable with one another, finding things they have in common, and are much more agreeable when potential stressors arise. This is especially true when everyone has the goal of harmony for the couple.

SCRIPTURE

> Let us then pursue what makes for peace and for mutual edification. (Romans 14:19)

In the context of wedding planning, "mutual edification" means cooperation and collaboration to make the big day special.

22

Who Pays for What?

THE SHOWER

Paying for the shower assumes one thing: the bride *wants* a shower. Most brides were surprised by a shower thrown by the bridal party and/or one or more of the parents. Nowadays, many brides don't want a shower—they want something different, or they want to be part of planning it. Once again, times have changed. Whether you're considering a traditional shower or something else, let's call it a "bride-to-be event," or BTBE for short.

Scenario 1. The bride may decide what she wants, and everyone else—the bridal party, parents, siblings, and others—may cooperatively plan the event and, hopefully, determine who is going to pay for it. The BTBE could be a simple affair in someone's home or a much more elaborate party at a venue. Some brides may want the groom and other men involved.

While the cost of the shower was traditionally borne by the bridal party, it certainly doesn't have to be that way. Once the bride has expressed what she wants, the bridal party and parents should make decisions about:

- who will pay for it
- who will be the point person
- who will do what

The point person will act as a liaison with the bride and work with her to determine how she envisions the BTBE. Remember that the goal is always to alleviate stress for the bride, and having another event to deal with could be an additional source of stress.

Scenario 2. Alternatively, you could plan a traditional bridal shower where the pressure on the bride is nonexistent because she is not involved in the overall planning. All she has to do is provide a guest list and show up.

In scenario 2, the bride lets go of the reins and allows family and friends to plan the shower and even make it a surprise. By not involving herself in the planning, the bride shows how much she trusts her family and friends and how grateful she is for whatever BTBE they arrange.

Surprise bridal showers can also include the groom and even other men, like the dads and friends of the groom. The groom can provide information about the bride's schedule, gift registry ideas, photos, and insights regarding games and favors. The groom will probably know or can find out if the bride would like a surprise.

REFLECTION

Most brides generally agree that the bride should express what she wants and let the moms/friends/bridal party plan the event.

THE WEDDING

Ah, life used to be simple. Back in the day, the bride's parents paid for pretty much everything, with the groom's parents chipping in for things like the rehearsal dinner and perhaps flowers. Today, who pays for what depends mostly on the financial situations of all involved.

In the past, parents paid and made the rules, and couples appreciated their help. Today, parents don't usually lead—instead, they play electronic catch-up to the likes of Google, Facebook, X, Instagram, Pinterest, and many other social media sites.

Some weddings are more traditional, where the parents of the bride cover most or even all the costs. Sometimes the other parents help, or the couple themselves can contribute. With the bride's parents covering the bill, did they get "more of what they wanted" because they were paying? This is sometimes the case.

Some parents we know faced a situation where the couple wanted/insisted on paying for their wedding, giving them total control over the amount they spent and what they spent it on. This approach can be particularly attractive when the parents are retired and on a fixed income. In such instances the couple makes enough money to pay for the entire wedding.

A third approach is when the parents of the bride split the costs equally with the groom's parents, making this a truly cooperative method. Of course, this assumes that both sets of parents are financially capable of committing half the costs. An honest conversation among all is necessary to establish a projected budget.

A rather unique approach we encountered was one where the parents got together and decided to give the happy couple a lump sum that they could spend as they wished. Each set of parents gave as much as they could afford. One reason the couple liked this approach was that they could spend the money on the wedding any way they wanted to: they could save thousands by going with a DJ instead of a live band; they could scale down the event and use some of the money as a down payment on a house; or they could splurge everything on the wedding day. The key is that the couple could make these financial decisions without any undue pressure from the parents.

Of course, there are many other approaches that combine some of these elements. What's critically important in any of these scenarios is open and honest communication. The couple should be open with all the parents involved as to what is important to them and their futures. And parents should continue to do their part to ensure a smooth prewedding process. After all, enjoyment of the day is the goal. Removing financial obstacles through open communication is a great way to do this.

REFLECTION

For many couples, it is about finding the right balance between their desires and the wishes of those who are paying in whole or in part for the wedding. A recurring theme is that a little compromise never hurt anybody. One couple we spoke to chose to pay for everything so they did not feel beholden to the parents. While they were happy with that decision, they did incorporate things that they knew were important to their parents.

SPECIAL EVENTS

Weddings can turn into two- or three-day celebrations with activities, afterparties, and next-day breakfasts. Planning for and orchestrating the additional events allows the couple to work with the parents to make the entire experience wonderful.

With every event or activity in addition to the reception, stress and conflict can easily rear their ugly heads. Do the bride and groom and parents really need or want do deal with the extra detail and effort? Or do they view it all as something fun that doesn't feel like work? And then there's the cost. We've been invited to weddings that have included, among many other things, the following:

- a getting-to-know-everyone outdoor picnic or indoor party before the wedding
- a football game on the beach the night before the wedding
- an afterparty—anything from drinks in the hotel lobby to another round of food
- a prayer circle following the reception
- a hike in the mountains the day before
- a continental breakfast, buffet, or luncheon the next day

What's common among all these—and what remains the source of stress—is time and money.

Whether it's organizing that football game on the beach or throwing an afterparty to end all afterparties, the easiest way for the bride and groom to avoid stress is to decide what they want and then ask for help in planning and executing it. However, it's also good for parents to make suggestions if the couple is simply not considering all options due to so many other responsibilities.

Here's one approach: The couple discusses their vision for special events like they discussed their vision for their wedding, with their parents. That discussion, held far in advance, should result in determining who will pay for what and what the couples and parents will do. Then, the couple and their parents can solicit help from family and friends. This is a collaboration that should work in the same way that the bridal party works with the bride for the shower or BTBE.

If the idea is to have several events, look for people who have specific strengths and skill sets to help. For example, if the groom's best man is into outdoor activities, he may organize a hike as one of the events. He would be responsible for communicating the date, time, and what people should wear and bring. Perhaps the parents of the groom can handle the day-after breakfast or brunch.

The bride and groom should publicly recognize those who helped make these events possible. Planning these events sooner than later will eliminate plenty of stress.

REFLECTION

One couple whose family owned a summer camp organized several days of swimming, hiking, eating meals in the mess hall, and sitting around a campfire. They remembered it as a great way to enjoy people, especially those they didn't get to see often.

Couples look forward to these special events, including the breakfast the following morning, as a nice way to say "Thanks for coming to our wedding. We're glad you could make it." It also gives people an opportunity to talk in a more relaxed setting.

SCRIPTURE

> Owe no one anything, except to love one another,
> for the one who loves another has fulfilled the law.
> (Romans 13:8)

When the couple loves each other and their parents, families, and friends, problems are more easily resolved.

23

Attire

THE BRIDE

Choosing the right wedding dress is often preceded by fifty to a hundred uncertainties. Making the "final decision" can sometimes be a long and difficult process for the bride. Hopefully, the following suggestions can help make it enjoyable for the bride-to-be, parents, or others the bride has invited.

Some brides will seek the opinions of their mothers; others won't. Some will prefer input from bridesmaids, friends, and even dads, or any combination of these. There's potential for many differing opinions and maybe a little disappointment as well.

However, it's best to remember that the bride has been dreaming about the perfect dress, so it's important that she feels comfortable and excited about her selection. If the bride has asked the mother of the bride or groom to shop with her, it is obvious that she would appreciate her input. What may be very important for the moms to voice are some practical concerns:

- "I know how much you love to dance, but are you going to be able to dance in this dress?"
- "With all that beading, it looks so heavy. Remember, you're going to be wearing it for a very long time."

- "Is it hot under there? The last thing you want to do is sweat."
- "Consider that alterations for this dress will cost a small fortune."
- And our favorite: "How are you going to the bathroom in that dress? Seriously—you'll need an entourage."

No need to say more. You get the point. In the end, everyone wants the bride to be happy.

Brides to be married in a Catholic Church should keep in mind that parishes expect appropriate and modest attire out of respect for the sacred space and the nature of the sacramental encounter that will take place. This may include covering your shoulders for the Mass or ceremony. These expectations about attire extend to bridesmaids and to the mothers of the bride and groom. Couples should contact their parish for dress code information.

REFLECTION

Generally, brides are happy they have open minds and avoid focusing on one dress style or designer. In hindsight, they appreciate the suggestions from the bridal salon staff, friends, and the moms. They feel that being flexible and open to suggestions almost always enhances the process.

THE GROOM AND GROOMSMEN

When it comes to their tuxedos, most guys don't know what to do with so many choices, so the groom and his groomsmen might experience some stress when deciding what to wear. Figuring this out can be more difficult than just renting a simple black tux.

The groom could get stressed out when consulting with the bride for her input, then "selling" the result to his team. He has to consider that some of his guys may not have sufficient funds, whereas others might prefer to wear a tux or suit they already own rather than renting or buying a new one.

The couple and parents could find themselves at odds if they have different viewpoints on the general dress code. If it's a formal upscale wedding, tuxes for all men might be required. If it's a more casual wedding, suits might be more appropriate.

So, to alleviate stress and conflict about what the men in the bridal party should wear, the couple should consider all these factors and decide together, and then the groom and his groomsmen will know exactly what to wear.

It's then time to choose styles and colors if you've settled on something other than black. Have fun guys, and don't make this stressful when it doesn't have to be. After all, you're not shopping for a wedding dress.

REFLECTION

After hearing what the brides go through to choose their dresses, most grooms say they are happy not to be female. Some grooms state that their own personal style determines whether they choose tuxes or suits. They want to choose something they feel comfortable in and fits their personality.

THE BRIDESMAIDS

If you've watched the movie *27 Dresses*, you know what a big deal bridesmaid dresses can be, and not just for the bride. For some brides, what her bridesmaids wear is a big issue;

other brides are not as prescriptive. Here are three common scenarios based on our conversations with brides.

Bride 1 prefers a uniform look with her bridal party:

- The bride selects the dress color.
- Together the bride and bridesmaids choose the style (keeping price in mind).
- The bride feels strongly that they all wear the same dress, jewelry, and so on.
- The bride shops with her bridesmaids, but in most cases she's already made up her mind about the attire.

Bride 2 is more flexible and sensitive to her bridesmaids' needs, tastes, and budgets:

- The bride selects color scheme but allows bridesmaids to choose shades of that color that look best on them.
- The bride allows them to select the style that looks good on them.
- The bride requests the color of footwear but gives them freedom for styles.
- The bride considers what the bridesmaids can afford and shops accordingly.

Bride 3 is a free spirit whose only concern is to have those closest to her stand with her on her wedding day:

- The bride selects the color scheme, but the rest is up to the bridesmaids.
- The bride allows them to select the dress of choice—short or long, solid or print pattern.
- The bride has no restrictions on shoes.

- The bride gives her bridesmaids freedom of choice based on what they can afford.
- The bride communicates openly to ensure a cohesive look.

The first scenario carries the least risk in how the bridesmaids and bride will look together in their dresses, especially for the photos. However, there's no right answer, so the bride needs to consider carefully, perhaps with guidance from bridesmaids, the matron of honor, and the mothers of the bride and groom, in order to mitigate the greatest amount of stress.

In general, the more informal and relaxed the wedding, the more scenarios 2 and 3 make sense. However, for a black-tie affair, the first scenario is often preferred.

REFLECTION

Bridal party members really appreciate how the bride keeps their financial situations in mind, allowing them to choose colors and styles.

THE PARENTS

There's one "commandment" of wedding planning for the moms that every bride, mother of the bride, and mother of the groom can mostly agree on: "Thou shalt not wear white or ivory."

After that it can get murky fast, depending on the personalities.

The color scheme and style of the mothers' dresses/gowns is very important, especially for the pictures that will be around forever.

Clearly, no mother should upstage the bride, especially

when it comes to what they wear. We think that's understandable. Shopping for attire for the mothers is another opportunity for good bonding if the bride comes along. A few basic observations from brides and moms we've talked with include:

- The mothers' dresses should *complement* the bride's dress in style and color.
- Neutral colors—earth tones, gray, navy—work well.
- Mothers should not overdo the bling.
- It has become common practice that the mother of the bride gets first choice in selecting the color of her dress before the groom's mother.

So far so good, right?

A real stressor can arise when either mother wants to wear something loud, flashy, or patterned. For most brides, bright colors like red and orange are a big no. Revealing or other inappropriate styles should be avoided unless the bride agrees with it.

It's always advisable for the moms to ask what the bride has in mind, and then take that advice into consideration based on the mom's tastes. Brides typically have a good idea of what they want and discuss with the moms to come to an agreement.

Word to the wise: don't let this become a problem.

And what about the dads?

Piece of cake for sure. The attire for the fathers of the bride and groom should complement the formality of the event: a tux for formal, a dark suit for semiformal, and a lighter color for outdoor summer weddings.

A quick conversation with the dads about attire should be all you need.

REFLECTION

Most brides indicate that they are very happy when their moms ask for input on selecting their wedding dresses. It is a fun time and a great experience.

SCRIPTURE

> Wisdom is with those who take advice. (Proverbs 13:10)

When everyone involved in planning the wedding has an open mind and is willing to compromise, stress and conflict vanish and are replaced by joy, fun, and camaraderie.

24

Ask the Couple to Delegate

With so much to do, even the simplest tasks can fall through the cracks or be subject to the "too many cooks in the kitchen" problem.

Let's assume that parents, friends, and siblings will want to help plan and execute the best wedding and any special events surrounding the wedding day.

Based on successfully run organizations, *delegation* is key.

While it's important for the bride and groom to listen to opinions—whether they use them or not—they should (courteously) delegate specific tasks. For example:

- "Dad, can you make sure the DJ and the photographer have the exact information about where to go at the venue and what time to arrive, and can you express our wish list as we discussed?"
- "Mom, can you make sure everyone knows the dress fitting is Saturday at 10:00 a.m. and give people directions if they need them?"
- "Hey bro, I'm emailing you the venue contract. Can you let me know if any changes are needed?"

Prior to asking for specific help, the couple should convey exactly what they want to happen. To ensure that delegation works, it must be precise and detailed. Simply saying

"Dad, it would be great if you could please take care of the shuttle" is not enough and leaves room for error.

To make the wedding a success, the couple should allow their "inner circle" of family and friends to raise concerns about potential issues they may have not thought about and make suggestions. Making requests like "Would you like to come to the meeting with the venue?" or "Can you help with the shuttle?" is sensible. Those who do help should keep the couple informed and up to date.

It's a good idea for the couple to keep a simple list of who they asked to do what and email each helper so that they can keep the details in order. Make sure to ask everyone to report back.

REFLECTION

Couples say that their parents "fill in a lot of the blanks" by doing things that are based on their experiences and areas of expertise and are grateful for them catching those details that they overlook.

SCRIPTURE

> And can any of you by worrying add a single hour to your span of life? If then you are not able to do a small thing, why do you worry about the rest? (Luke 12:25–26)

Replace worrying with action, because worrying detracts from the joyous occasion that planning should be.

25

Assisting with Vendors

Parents, other family members, and friends can be a huge help to the couple in many ways, based primarily on their experiences and areas of expertise. Every task that the couple doesn't have to do means less stress for them.

As early as possible, make a list of all the potential ways people can help the couple in a collaborative effort so the wedding-planning process is a productive and stress-free experience.

It is very likely that the Catholic parents have already done many of the things that need to be done for a Catholic wedding. They may have helped plan a wedding for an older sibling, planned an anniversary party, or learned much from friends whose children are already married.

Here are examples of things to consider:

- The father of the bride owns a liquor store and could be a good source for buying liquor at wholesale prices; he may even feel inclined to donate.
- The groom's mom owns a Party City franchise, a potential source for favors and other needs, including for the afterparty.
- The groom's brother owns a print shop that could be a source for all the printed invitations, programs, shuttle schedules, and so on.

- The groom's dad is an attorney and could review the contracts.
- The bride's sister has a friend who is a wedding planner and could provide some free advice.
- The bride's mom is very creative and could make amazing centerpieces (approved by the couple).
- One of the bridesmaids works for a florist and may be able to get a good deal.
- One of the groom's cousins is a baker and could make the wedding cake.
- The bride's uncle just happens to be friends with the owner of a venue and can "pull some strings" to get the best deal.
- The groom's aunt is a therapist and can offer insight on the best way to deal with some annoying people that might cause angst.
- The groom's mother plans parties for her job and can suggest small details that will help the couple make decisions about such things as floral arrangements or the amount of food to order.

In addition to these specific tasks, parents can offer themselves as sounding boards as the couple looks at venues and talks with other vendors.

Essentially, couples should tap into the expertise of parents, other family members, and friends to get things done effectively and with minimal stress.

REFLECTION

Couples and their friends dread all the negotiations, contracts, insurance, and other necessary but un-fun stuff; consequently, they are thrilled when the parents volunteered to handle them.

26

Vendor Communications

You know what they say: "Keep your friends close and your wedding vendors closer."

Productive and respectful communication with your vendors is essential and will go a long way toward ensuring minimal stress and the best possible outcome on your wedding day.

While this day is one of the most important ones for the couple, it is one of many important days for your vendors. It's always good to remember that your goal and the vendor's goal is the same: they want their businesses to be successful by making sure your wedding is what you want. Mutual respect is a great asset in these relationships.

It's a good idea to set up a new email address dedicated only to wedding communications. This makes it easy to keep all wedding-related emails separate. It's also a good idea to allow guests to post questions and requests on your wedding platform.

When you start to talk with vendors, ask the following questions:

- How do they prefer to communicate?
- What is their usual response time?
- Do they have a timeframe/schedule for the responsibilities from start to end, preferably broken down by month?

Just as you want vendors to answer your questions promptly, you need to do so as well. And in the same way that you want vendors to be courteous and respectful to you, you need to do the same in return.

Choose one point of contact for each vendor. The last thing you want is for a vendor to become confused when more than one person contacts them. Make sure all parents know who the point person is, and tell the venue not to take calls from anyone else.

Before you choose each vendor, do your homework and ask for references. No vendor should resist this request. If they do, it may be for a good reason.

In many cases—for example, when you're looking for a florist, hair stylist, cake baker, or other vendor—a picture is worth a thousand words. It's a good idea to provide photos of what you like to enhance your written and verbal communications.

Always confirm every verbal conversation via email or text, such as "Thanks for your time today. We agreed that the sushi station would be included at no extra cost."

Of course, if a vendor isn't getting back to you in the timeframe that they originally committed to, you need to find out if there is an issue. Your contact may be sick, on vacation, or handling some other problem, so you need to deal with this sooner than later.

REFLECTION

One couple feared that the groom's mother would try to get involved in every minor detail, including calling the vendors. The groom was relieved that, after a discussion with his mom, she complied with their wishes to let them handle everything.

27

Negotiations and Contracts

When it comes to negotiating with wedding vendors, it's very important to be aware of the following criteria so as to obtain the best results:

- The couple and parents need to feel that the agreed-upon price for specific services is fair and the final price is locked in.
- The couple and parents need to recognize that the vendor is entitled to make a fair profit and has the right to refuse to work with anybody.

It must be a win-win outcome. Knowing that, let's use the venue/caterer as an example, although you must consider the following in negotiations with every vendor:

- Determine the budget for the venue, food, and drink.
- Take the budget and divide it by the number of probable attendees to get a price per person (or per plate as it is called).
- Search for venues that fit into the general per-plate range that you can afford, and make sure you do an apples-to-apples comparison based on the venue, the quality and amount of food,

and how much liquor (and which brands) will be served.

- Determine who has the most experience in negotiating and consider letting that person lead the conversation with the venue.

One example that we encountered: the couple and parents figured out what they could afford per plate. The venue presented several packages at different price points. The father of the groom led the talks with the venue's representative, knowing the bottom line ahead of time.

When the contract was presented, everyone reviewed it and requested some changes to clarify points. One important clause that the groom's father insisted on, and that the couple had not thought about, was how to handle an unavoidable event, like a tornado or fire, that rendered the venue unusable. The father also "redlined" the contract to make sure some of the points were clear and not ambiguous.

One of the vendors did not have a contract, so the father found one online, modified it, and discussed it with the vendor in question.

With everything stated clearly, the family left no room for misunderstandings.

REFLECTION

Couples express their appreciation for help in this area but also feel it is essential to review what is agreed upon with each vendor.

28

Venue and Catering

Since the venue and catering will be the most expensive part of the wedding, it's important to minimize stress within the family and with the venue/caterer (combined here since most venues offer catering).

First, the couple and parents need to be prepared when meeting with the venue/caterer. This means being "buttoned up" regarding what you want and presenting it professionally. The more professional you are, the better the relationship will be here and with any vendor. You want the vendor to come away saying, "I love working with these people."

Before you meet in person, make sure that you have reviewed all information about the venue/caterer online and any printed information you have requested. Look at the pictures, see if there are any online complaints or reviews, and understand their packages, terms, and conditions. Most venues now post this information online.

Remember that, while your big day is the main thing that's important to you, the venue/caterer will be very busy working with other brides and grooms and clients. Learning how best to work with them is of paramount importance.

Assuming your Catholic wedding Mass or ceremony is taking place in your parish church, make sure that the reception venue is aware that they are not responsible for the ceremony. If your vendor charges a specific fee for the wedding ceremony, you should be able to deduct it from total venue expenses. If the wedding ceremony fee is included in the overall package, you should negotiate for an appropriate discount or substitution.

One thing all vendors will appreciate is asking, "What is the best way to contact you: phone, email, or text?"

This simple question shows them that you are professional and that you respect how they work best (see chapter 26, "Vendor Communications"). Make sure that their answers to your questions are clear and unambiguous. If you don't understand something, ask them to clarify it. Remember, the devil is in the details. Take extensive notes on what they verbally agree to, and make sure the contract reflects those commitments. Talk with the vendor about the fun and cool things you've seen at other weddings or found online.

Show your appreciation for their time and expertise with a warm thank-you, and once you decide to book a given venue/caterer, contact them in the preferred manner and express your desire to work closely to ensure a wonderful event.

REFLECTION

If the contact at the venue/caterer changes due to illness or some other reason, vendors who take copious notes are thankful that they had done so. While the replacements are generally aware of the wedding plans, the notes ensure that the replacement and the couple are on the same page.

"I WISH WE HAD THOUGHT OF THAT"

After the reception, what happens to all the leftover food, centerpieces, gifts, and anything else that you have paid for and doesn't belong to the venue?

Essentially, it's your responsibility. You need to assemble a team of people and vehicles to help carry out everything you want to take.

Of course, ask if the venue can pack up food that you and your "clean-up" team can take. You certainly don't want precious memories tossed away because you didn't take them.

29

Accommodations and Transportation

When it comes to Catholic weddings that typically take place in a church, arranging transportation is different from weddings where all events take place at the reception venue. It might be helpful to refer to "The Wedding Day" section in part 1 to make sure you consider accommodation and transportation at all events on your wedding day.

Once the hotel(s) is chosen and transportation to and from the venue is arranged, these two items are forgotten until things go wrong on the wedding day. Shuttle service is sometimes a freebie from the hotel, and as such, you're basically leaving it up to them that all guests will arrive in time for the church ceremony. From our personal experience, much can go wrong, and something usually does.

First, let's consider the hotel. Make sure you get a written confirmation of the number of rooms that are being set aside for your wedding, the discounted rate, and the deadline by which they must be booked before they are released.

Insist that they put up your signs advising guests where and at what times to pick up the shuttle, and ensure that all front desk staff are knowledgeable about the transportation, even if they did not arrange it. At one hotel, no one could tell us when the shuttle would depart and where to meet it, and we had to walk around in the rain to find it. That is a stressful experience for guests.

Second, let's consider the transportation. While the promise of one shuttle making the fifteen-minute drive back and forth several times to pick up guests sounds good, that plan can go awry:

- People are slow to board the shuttle, especially older folks.
- The driver insists on waiting for every seat to be filled before departing.
- There are traffic or construction delays on the way.
- People beg the driver to wait for one more person or to squeeze on two more people.
- There is an accident blocking the roadway.
- The shuttle is too small to accommodate the number of guests at the hotel.

Being proactive may be the answer to most of these issues. Talking to whomever is providing transportation and getting their responses about these issues gives you a clear understanding on how they handle them. Even if you must pay extra for a second vehicle, you don't want guests to miss the ceremony. Find out how many rooms must be booked to get the free shuttle service and how many people the shuttle holds. Divide the shuttle capacity by the number of guests to find how many trips the shuttle will need to make. *Plan accordingly.*

For the return to the hotel after the wedding reception, arrange for signs or slips of paper on each table that confirms the departure times and the location of the return shuttle. An announcement by the band or DJ is another consideration.

On the day of the wedding, someone needs to call the hotel and transportation provider to make sure everything is on schedule and that signs have been posted. If you sign a contract directly with the entity providing the transportation, build in an extra half hour after the wedding so that guests are not left stranded at the venue. Nothing runs like clockwork, especially if transportation is needed from the hotel to the church, from the church to pre-reception activities, then to the reception venue, and then back to the hotel.

One way around the transportation issue is to book a hotel within walking distance of the venue or church. But you would still need to make special "what-if" arrangements if rain or snow is in the forecast. You especially don't want elderly or disabled people walking in bad weather. Book sufficient transportation early in the process to ensure that there are enough vehicles based on the estimated number of guests.

REFLECTION

We've heard about shuttle delays that caused people to miss the ceremony more often than you'd think. Generally, the couples feel that they could have done more to ensure that these problems didn't happen by booking earlier.

30

Seating Arrangements

Take two aspirins and let's put together a seating chart with as little pain as possible. This should be one of the least stressful aspects of wedding planning, but it often is not, and it can often take more time than it should. For example, Aunt Millie isn't speaking with Uncle Willie, and the Hatfield and McCoy families can't be near each other. That's where we need to start! Make a list of seating considerations, along these lines:

- Group families together.
- Due to the volume, seat elderly people away from the band or DJ speakers.
- Group friends of the bride and groom together in one area.
- Make notes on people who should not be seated at the same table or even near one another.
- Consider where single guests will feel most comfortable.
- Determine if there will be one table for small children, one for teens.

One way to proceed is for the couple to take a crack at doing the entire chart and then showing it to their parents. Ask the venue for a room layout as that will be very helpful.

Another way is for the bride and groom to assign the seating for their friends and allow the parents to assign the seating for their respective families, friends, and co-workers. Once completed, the layout should be reviewed and accepted or discussed further.

What happens when there are conflicts that have no immediate resolution?

One solution is for the parents to resolve any issues with people whom they are responsible for seating. So, therefore, the bride's parents, not the bride and groom, deal with Aunt Millie and Uncle Willie. This straightforward approach gets the bride and groom out of the middle of sticky situations.

Many venues have tables of different sizes and shapes that can seat different numbers of guests. Before spending time on the seating chart, confirm the table options so that all those involved have the correct information. Usually, tables can seat from four to fifteen people, so find out how many of each table the venue has.

To reduce stress when trying to figure out seating, consider an online tool like prismm.com that makes it easy for everyone to manage planning and collaboration.

REFLECTION

Some couples remembered that this was one of the most difficult tasks they faced. They wanted everyone to feel comfortable and enjoy the people at their table.

We learned that proactive couples chose to give a quick call, email, or text ahead of time to let some people know who they would be sitting with and why. They felt that this simple heads-up went a long way toward making people feel comfortable sitting with those they have never met.

SCRIPTURE

> Jesus and his disciples had also been invited to the wedding. When the wine gave out, the mother of Jesus said to him, "They have no wine." (John 2:2)

Mary asked Jesus to help the couple at the wedding reception in Cana. You too can ask for help from him, and he will assist you.

31

The Big Day

THE CEREMONY

To the bride and groom: this is one of the most important days of your life. The time has finally come to celebrate your wedding in the presence of God and those who have loved and supported you over the years. The beautiful rituals of your Catholic wedding will reflect the sacredness of the promises you will make today and for the rest of your lives. Keep focused and hold onto every moment. You deserve this!

The wedding vows that you will recite to each other before God, your family, friends, and parish community will be among the most important words you will ever voice. Each word has great meaning, and it's important to reflect on them in the days and hours before the wedding. Keep a copy of your vows close and read them regularly as they will be an inspiration throughout your lives.

Imagining Your Catholic Wedding Day

You each wake up early with the sunrise and thank God for the wonderful day. At last, it is your wedding day! You are still basking in the glory of the events of the night before. First, the rehearsal, where your closest friends and family shared in your delight as they practiced their various roles for the nuptial Mass (or ceremony). The priest began by inviting your entire wedding party to pray for you as a couple in preparation for the sacred bond of matrimony—to be celebrated the next day and then forever. You even had the opportunity to receive the sacrament of reconciliation in preparation for the wedding, and you both have an amazing sense of peace.

Then came the rehearsal dinner where the two families and your group of special friends gathered in your honor. You were each celebrated as individuals who will soon become one. You were toasted as a couple over and over with enormous happiness and anticipation.

Now that you're awake, you think of each other as you begin your day with so much to do, but you know that all the hard work and challenging moments of planning were worth it. Now it is in God's hands.

As the bride, you look forward to the day—the makeup and hair for you and your wedding party, spending precious moments with your mom (or anyone else you're close to), who has been there for you along the way, allowing yourself to be pampered and be the center of attention as you think about what it must have been like for Mary, our Blessed Mother, on her wedding day.

As the groom, you enjoy your first cup of coffee and think about your friends and family, especially your siblings who grew up with you and know all about you, but mostly your parents, who have given the world to you. You consider the sacrifices they have always made for you and think of Jesus on the cross—the ultimate sign of sacrificial love.

Now, you arrive separately at the church. For the bride, it's her spiritual home, the parish where she received her sacraments and religious education, her family of families. For the groom, it is the place where your faith came alive as you both shared the Eucharist as boyfriend and girlfriend and eventually as the future bride and groom.

Together, you've made the decision to have a nuptial Mass, an appropriate celebration of marriage between two

Catholics. The first meal you will share as a married couple is the Eucharist. Jesus is your source of unity. You have invited Jesus to your wedding and to be an integral part of your marriage each day.

After a beautiful Mass filled with the rituals of your Catholic faith, you are filled with God's grace and an overabundance of love. As your family and friends go to various gatherings in anticipation of the wedding reception, you have some quiet time together to pray in thanksgiving.

Once again, you gather with family and friends, who have already arrived at your reception and are ready to celebrate with you. You see nothing but happy faces. You've brought joy and new life to this community gathered in your honor. Now it's time for the feast—food, fun, abundant wine, laughter, music, dancing, and so much love, just like the wedding feast at Cana where Jesus's first miracle occurred. Your wedding day is celebrated on earth and in heaven. God has made *two become one*!

Some Thoughts on Marriage and the Eucharist

> The spirituality of family love is made up of thousands of small but real gestures that bring together the real and the divine, for it is filled with the love of God. In the end, marital spirituality is a spirituality of the bond in which God dwells.
>
> Pope Francis

By deciding to get married, you are taking a leap of faith that you will love and honor each other forever, but because we are all human, you will have times when loving and honoring can be difficult. That's when we say that love is a decision, an act of the will, not just a feeling. That's what we call *sacrificial, self-giving* love, and sometimes that requires superhuman ability.

As Christians, we know that Jesus's love was the ultimate self-giving love. He willingly suffered and gave his life for us so that we might have eternal life. In the Eucharist, not only do we recall what Jesus did for us, but through the power of the Holy Spirit and the action of the priest, Jesus's sacrifice also becomes fully present in real time:

> The whole Christ is truly present—body, blood, soul, and divinity—under the appearances of bread and wine, the glorified Christ who rose from the dead. This is what the Church means when she speaks of the "Real Presence" of Christ in the Eucharist. ("The Eucharist," United States Conference of Catholic Bishops)

In the prayers of consecration at Mass, we hear the priest repeating the words of Jesus at the Last Supper, "Take this, all of you, and eat of it: for this is my Body which will be given up for you."

When we consider the connection between marriage and the Eucharist, there are five things to keep in mind:

1. In marriage, we promise to give ourselves freely, totally, faithfully, and forever (until death) to our husband/wife, just as Jesus gives himself to us freely, totally, faithfully, and forever in the Eucharist. Through the Eucharist we can say we have a spousal (marital) relationship with Jesus.
2. In the Eucharist Jesus becomes one with us—he enters our body and penetrates our soul. He is our true *soulmate* just like married couples are to each other.

3. There are times when our self-giving love in marriage and parenthood leaves us physically and emotionally spent; we give it our all! This is when we are saying with our actions, "This is my body given up for you."
4. The Eucharist is the source and summit of our faith. This means that, when we receive the Eucharist and are fully united with Christ, we become fully charged with his energy, like a battery, to meet the daily demands of marriage and family life.
5. Jesus is the source of all healing, forgiveness, faith, hope, trust, and love—Jesus *is* our superpower. We simply can't live out our marriage without him! On your wedding day, Jesus gives you the grace to be married; throughout your marriage, Jesus gives you the grace to live it out.

THE RECEPTION

It's a given that Murphy's Law (anything that can go wrong, will) always seems to strike at the worst time—including the wedding day. You should be prepared for anything, and how you respond to whatever it is that goes wrong is more important than anything else.

Either the couple, a parent, or a "go-to" person whom you have delegated should take charge and work toward finding a solution to any problems that occur. The following real-life stories demonstrate how some creative thinking can turn lemons into lemonade.

- Guests were gathering outside the church for the wedding when the priest informed the wedding planner that there was an accidental double booking and that a funeral procession would be arriving in minutes. The quick-thinking planner saw an ice cream truck parked a short walk away and arranged for all the guests to enjoy a sweet treat until the church became available. (See ArtofCelebrations.com.)

- A family friend was supposed to do makeup but bailed at the last minute. Luckily, the hair stylist was able to call in a team that happened to be nearby, and they came and saved the day. This happens more often than people think, so make sure you have a Plan B. (See BeautyEntourage .com.)
- When a zipper on his bride's dress broke, a groom spent a good half hour holding the dress closed and calming her as someone sewed it up. Make sure you have an emergency kit for these kinds of mishaps. (See GracefulHost.com.)
- A couple insisted on a tented outdoor reception on a farm, but the day before the tent was to be installed, it poured, turning the area to mud. Luckily, the owner of the farm allowed the barn to be used for the reception. In preparation for the celebration, the groom and his groomsmen cleaned out the stalls and spread fresh hay on the ground.
- The florist was late due to heavy traffic on a holiday weekend and, to make matters worse, delivered the wrong flowers. The bride hated her bouquet. The planner jumped into action and, with permission of the venue management, made a new bouquet using garden roses and foliage from inside and outside the premises. (CharmedEventsPlanning.com.)

- Besides being two hours late, the baker had dropped the wedding cake and tried to put it back together. It was missing two layers and looked awful. The planner surrounded the wounded cake with a lot of flowers and turned the spotlights down. The venue chipped in with extra desserts to take the focus off the cake. (alliey.co.)

When choosing vendors, ask them "what if" questions based on the above examples. See how quickly they come up with solutions. One unexpected situation was that some of the gifts for the couple disappeared. While most presents were envelopes with checks, there were a handful of gifts in boxes. Maybe the "go-to" person could periodically put boxes and gift bags in a car for safekeeping.

REFLECTION

Those couples who make up their minds ahead of time that nothing is going to bother them won't be fazed when the DJ has a technical issue and the best man rambles for too long. They are determined to not let anything stand in the way of a great time.

SCRIPTURE

> The human mind plans the way, but the LORD directs the steps. (Proverbs 16:9)

Plan your wedding, and let God show you how to minimize stress and conflict.

32

Wedding Day Honors

THE CEREMONY

It's probably true that everyone who attends the wedding Mass or ceremony would love to have a role or honor, but only a small portion expects it. The couple knows who should get an honor—parents, siblings, relatives, and friends. The couple usually makes their choice of honors on the strength of the relationship they have with each person being considered.

But what about others who *think* they should have some form of honor, but the couple doesn't agree?

For Catholic weddings, since the wedding Mass or ceremony follows a particular order, only certain people can be given special roles in the wedding (see "Planning Your Wedding Ceremony," in part 1).

The list of honors includes ushers for seating and handing out programs, readers, and gift bearers for the offertory procession. For others outside of the bridal party, the couple should consider different ways of making people feel honored by giving them a special role in the pre-reception activities or those at the reception.

The idea is to acknowledge certain people and make them feel great about being part of the day. Couples should keep in mind that friendships change over time.

Perhaps someone that you would consider for an honor today may not be someone you'd choose a year down the road, or vice versa. Consequently, there's no need to rush into most honors. Wait until later in the process.

> The love we feel for another person leads to the love of God, and robes us in garments of light.
>
> Rabbi Jonathan Sacks,
> "The Garments of Light"

THE RECEPTION

In the same way the couple can honor people during the ceremony, they can also follow the same philosophy for the reception. The potential stress of not including someone is dramatically reduced by including more people. In addition, granting special honors makes the wedding reception even more memorable. For example, invite someone:

- to lead the blessing before the meal at the reception (ask your parish for an appropriate prayer)
- to read a poem or special reflection as part of the blessing
- to sing a special song or play a musical reflection
- to assist in preparing a traditional unity candle blessing at the reception
- to give a "brief toast" in addition to the traditional toasts (We've been to weddings where the couple, parents, or the bandleader/DJ invites *anyone* to say a *few* words, either live or recorded via video, that can be screened later during the reception.)
- to do a "spotlight dance" ("Now let's welcome the bride and her grandpa to the dance floor." The band/DJ can fade out after a minute, but the memory will last forever.)

- to set up a remembrance table where those who are no longer with us are honored (The bandleader/DJ can let people know about it by saying that "the couple wants everyone to know about the remembrance table to honor those special people who are not with us anymore." For people who have recently passed, a moment of silence can be very special.)

These are just a few potential reception honors. We're sure the couple and parents would enjoy dreaming up additional ones. Like many of the suggestions throughout this book, these are designed to build family harmony, long-lasting friendships, and special moments that will be remembered long after the wedding day.

REFLECTION

On reflection, a couple regretted not highlighting a few close people at the reception beyond the traditional honors. The couple recognized that people appreciate being acknowledged when they are close to the bride or groom and wished they had done more.

33

The Wedding Planner

From the first day until the wedding day, the staggering number of details that need to be addressed seems more difficult and time-consuming than climbing Mount Everest. That's why hiring a wedding planner—sometimes called a wedding coordinator—can make a good deal of sense for everyone, not just the couple.

At $1,500 to $3,000—or even more—nationally, planners can take on much of the nitty-gritty, leaving the couple and parents to do more of the fun stuff. Planners also offer flexible pricing based on the amount of work they do. People at the venue can also take on some of the work a planner does.

If you can afford a wedding planner, it's generally a good idea to hire one, considering the massive amount of detail involved in planning the wedding day. Furthermore, these professionals can also offer suggestions and a comprehensive timeline. Unless the couple *wants* to do most of the work themselves, a planner could mean the difference between long hours of preparation coupled with wedding-day annoyances and a much easier time.

Parents should also be involved with the wedding planner, especially on the big day. Since issues inevitably arise, the planner should ideally come to the parents or designated contact with any problems rather than inconveniencing the couple. The bride and groom will appreciate the assistance.

Planners also handle all the logistics—securing contracts, making sure everything is there on time, suggesting vendors, and even negotiating with vendors for discounted rates. Sometimes the wedding planner's fee, or a portion of it, could be paid by the money saved through the planner's tips and suggestions.

While vendors may enjoy working directly with couples, they likely prefer working with industry professionals who can save them time and headaches. Planners have vendors whom they trust and with whom they have worked, thereby eliminating potential problems from unknown and untested companies.

For Catholic weddings there is often someone from the parish designated to take care of the details of the nuptial Mass or ceremony. Your wedding planner should be supportive of the Catholic Mass or ceremony and should feel comfortable working with the parish wedding coordinator. If you're using a wedding planner, make sure the parish wedding coordinator and the wedding planner are aware of each other's roles and are on the same page.

REFLECTION

Those who can afford a wedding planner feel very lucky, as the planner helps keep them organized and accomplishes many things in a timely manner. When they can't decide on something, the planner often gives the couple another fresh perspective that helps foster the decision-making process.

On the day of the wedding, planners handle any problems that arise, some of which the couple don't even know about until after the affair. Many couples note that, if you can afford it and you know of a good, professional wedding planner, it's the way to go.

One bride we spoke to opted not to use a wedding planner. She felt she'd be making the final decisions anyway and didn't see the need. It should be noted that this bride was *very* organized. The couple knew exactly what they wanted and started the process about a year and half before the wedding.

34

Avoiding Common Problems

Wise and experienced parents can often spot red flags a mile away—problems that can threaten to get between the couple, and problems that can become theirs too if they are caught in the middle. Responsible parents will be proactive and help the couple get back on the right track with each other. Specifically, parents should be on the lookout for these telltale signs:

- One partner leaves all the planning and work to the other.
- The bride and groom are on different pages regarding a realistic budget.
- The couple is having a difficult time communicating with each other. How couples communicate can be very enlightening. Helping them through it is invaluable assistance for planning the wedding and ensuring a successful marriage.
- The couple has a hard time agreeing on major issues. If you observe this, then reviewing their vision for the big day (see chapter 1) is a good way to remind them to see the other's point of view, leading to compromise.
- There's a lack of respect between the couple. When one suggests something, the other might

say "That's a bad idea!" instead of "OK, let's talk about it and see where it leads."

Parents can help their daughter or son deal with common problems that could be red flags for the future of the relationship. Minor squabbles can occur over anything, from the color of linens to what desserts to have. When major issues arise and the couple is at a stalemate, it may be the right time for parents to:

- suggest that professional help, such as a therapist, mediator, or religious person, might be needed
- suggest that they play a bigger role in helping the couple figure things out

In any case, parents can remind their son or daughter that in serious situations, the embarrassment of a broken engagement is much easier to deal with and get over than a heartbreaking divorce. In many cases, a couple who constantly fights and disagrees may know that the marriage isn't going to work. Getting them to seek help to make a hard decision (to separate) sooner than later is the goal.

The good news for Catholic couples is that the marriage preparation process gives them the skills to resolve difficult issues. It also helps couples determine on their own when their issues are serious enough to postpone the wedding or end the relationship.

REFLECTION

Couples that seek the guidance of parents, a religious person, and friends find it helpful to "break the logjam" on the way to making good decisions.

35

Wedding Insurance

None of us knew that wedding insurance even existed. We've all heard horror stories about venues refusing to return deposits, expensive wedding dresses being delayed due to supply chain issues, and even wedding salons going out of business, leaving brides high and dry. If only we knew about wedding insurance. We wish that we had heard of Wedsure.com earlier.

Hopefully, most of us have learned from the COVID-19 pandemic. Wedding insurance is an inexpensive way to cover liability, cancellation, and even "change of heart." It turns out you can purchase several coverages:

- liability insurance that covers accidents and mishaps (often required by venues)
- cancellation insurance (just like it sounds)
- change of heart insurance (covers just that but may have to be purchased far in advance)
- special attire insurance (covers problems with wedding dresses)
- coverage for losses such as deposits and photographs

As with any insurance, check out what is and isn't covered, how much it costs, and what the claims process is, and record any other questions you've undoubtedly asked when purchasing insurance in the past. Generally, unexpected issues such as fire, hurricanes, tornados, and floods may be covered, but some issues, such as those related to pandemics, may not.

You won't have to purchase numerous different policies because companies such as Wedsure include nine coverages in one policy.

From our experience, it is our view that wedding insurance may be one thing the couple will agree to "absolutely." Parents can offer to research it. Should anything unforeseen happen, however, it's money well spent.

Another thing you must insure is the engagement ring, if you haven't already done so.

REFLECTION

Very few couples or parents we spoke to even knew about wedding insurance. Many couples experienced losses themselves and knew others who had setbacks due to things like hurricanes and tornados. While they got through it, they all said that, had they known about wedding insurance, they would have made the investment.

36

Having a Plan B

The pandemic caught everyone by surprise: couples, venues, vendors—no one was spared. While you can't foresee or plan for everything, if there is one critical lesson that couples and parents can learn now, it's that you have to have a *Plan B* for the major expenses.

No one could ever have predicted a pandemic of this nature, but there may be other wedding-planning trainwrecks just waiting to happen:

- tornados, earthquakes, floods, and other forces of nature
- power outages
- vendors who go out of business for a wide range of reasons
- overseas items (e.g., wedding dresses) whose shipment is delayed
- vendor employees and gig workers who become sick and can't make it on the wedding day
- guests canceling at the last minute or uninvited guests showing up
- printer mishaps with invitations and seating cards

While issues like these could derail any wedding plans, if you create a Plan B, you minimize the stress and financial losses associated with these events.

Start by asking each vendor what *their* Plan B is. For example:

- Does your venue have backup generators in case of a power outage?
- If you get sick, do you have a colleague or partner who can take photos?
- If my dress gets delayed, what will you do?

Planning your wedding should be a very special and enjoyable experience, but it doesn't hurt to have the mindset that something may go wrong and that you might have to roll with the punches. Even if nothing happens, being prepared will give you peace of mind and reduce stress.

Creating a Plan B is an important discussion for all stakeholders, as you can draw on everyone's experiences to determine how best to deal with setbacks and changes.

While wedding insurance (see chapter 35) would not likely have covered COVID-related losses, it would have probably covered many of the items listed above.

Regarding attendance at the wedding ceremony or reception, you'll need to consider *any* health problems, especially if they are contagious and/or require vaccination.

REFLECTION

We found out that issues like COVID-19 can be anything from annoying inconveniences to major disasters for couples planning weddings. We also heard that the way couples and parents reacted to things out of their control was important, and getting through them together made it easier to deal with any issues that arose.

37

Guests Can Be Stressed Too

You think that you're the only ones who can be stressed on the wedding day? Think twice. The bad news is that guests can get stressed for a variety of reasons. The good news is that almost all their stress can be easily prevented. Here are a few examples:

Shuttle delays. This happens often, where shuttles between hotels and venues are delayed, sometimes resulting in guests missing the ceremony (see chapter 29, "Accommodations and Transportation"). Make sure you don't leave this arrangement totally up to the hotel or shuttle service. You need to be involved, as you would with any other service.

Older guests being seated too close to the band/DJ speakers. Not only does this cause difficulty for people hearing one another talk, loud volumes can be damaging to older ears. In addition to considering this when creating the seating chart (see chapter 30, "Seating Arrangements"), ask the bandleader/DJ to keep the volume at a reasonable level to facilitate conversation.

Sitting with other unfamiliar guests. While there will be some cases where this is unavoidable, familiarity with other guests makes for a more enjoyable time and reduces stress.

Rambling speeches and toasts. One of our couples made it very clear that we should keep toasts under five minutes and requested that all speakers practice their talks. This avoids the potential for boring and unrehearsed toasts and increases the likelihood that those given will be fast-moving and enjoyable.

Lack of communication. Guests may become upset when they have not been made aware of:

- the dress code for the event
- the preferred hotels with transportation to the venue
- a cash bar versus an open bar
- the starting times for both the ceremony and reception
- the shuttle times to and from the venue, and where to meet the shuttle
- the dates, times, and locations of any special events, like a next-day breakfast
- clear directions to all locations

Inconvenient date(s). Did you accidentally choose Super Bowl Sunday or a major religious holiday for the wedding? That will most definitely cause stress for some guests.

The time between the ceremony and the reception. A mid-morning ceremony or Mass followed by an evening reception leaves guests with many hours to fill. The bride and groom should plan pre-reception events, provide suggestions for activities, or take suggestions or offers from friends and family. They can post these suggestions and events on their wedding site so that guests can plan appropriately.

These potential stresses are easy to alleviate.

REFLECTION

We heard from several couples that guests staying at hotels were stressed out over shuttle arrival and departure times. That was the last thing couples wanted to hear on their wedding day. In retrospect, they realized that they could have coordinated better with the hotel staff, making it easy for them to inform guests of shuttle times and locations.

38

Relieving Stress on the Big Day

All those months of planning, and the wedding day has finally arrived. But couples everywhere are keeping their fingers crossed that nothing goes wrong.

It is likely that something will, but the most important point is to not let it ruin the day. Here are some ideas.

Assign one or more "go-to" people who are happy to handle any issues that arise. They can be guests or people who work for the venue. Let the manager(s) at the venue know who your personal "go-to" people are so that they can talk to them instead of you. Here's what the "go-to" people can handle:

- guests who are unhappy with the food or drink
- children who are making too much noise and misbehaving
- bringing boxed gifts out to a car for safekeeping
- ushering people to their seats
- asking people not to talk during the ceremony or speeches
- alerting staff when chafing dishes are running low
- working with staff if a table is short a place setting or a seat change is needed

If you're working with a wedding planner and/or coordinator (Note: while these two roles are slightly different, to most people they are interchangeable), managers from the venue, or caterer, supply them in advance with a list of what to do in certain cases. One family assumed that the venue would save personal items when breaking down the room, but they threw away the bride's bouquet and other personal items. While this should not happen, it's better to be safe than sorry by addressing such things before the wedding.

If you haven't dealt with the issue of shuttles getting everyone to the ceremony on time (see chapter 29), it's important to do that prior to the day of the event. The last thing you want is for people to arrive late. Remember, venues and officiants are usually on a schedule and may not be able to wait for those who are delayed; and if the ceremony is delayed, it can affect the reception as well.

The week before the wedding day, contact all vendors to ensure everything is on schedule according to previous communications. It's up to you to confirm all is well, and if there is a hitch, you'll still have time to fix it.

Two weeks before, make sure you contact any people who have not responded so that you can adjust the final count, if necessary, and potentially avoid paying too much and dealing with the stress of last-minute changes.

Ensure that all vendors are paid in full prior to or on the big day, and if you are planning on tipping any of the vendors, get cash for tip envelopes that are clearly labeled and given to someone (perhaps the best man) or one of the "go-to" people to distribute at the end of the evening.

Make sure to remember the wedding bands and, of course, something old, something new, something borrowed, and something blue.

Part III

THRIVE

The Future

Lessons Learned

For those who have been through the wedding-planning process, you'll likely agree with couples who say that planning is like a "boot camp" for the rest of their lives.

What you experience in planning a wedding will be almost identical to what you experience throughout your marriage—the circumstances will be different, of course:

- dealing with difficult people
- making good decisions
- learning to communicate and collaborate
- considering the feelings of others
- finding the right balance between what you want and what others desire

These "life skills" will come in handy every day of your lives, and learning from what you experience during the planning of your wedding will give you a good head start.

What's Really at Stake?

In addition to being an emotionally trying time, a wedding is one of the five most costly expenses a couple will plan for in their lifetime. When you combine all the costs—venue, caterer, flowers, dress, and so on—there's a great deal at stake. But as important as money is, it's a relatively small factor that you'll encounter when compared to...

Besides the money and stress, what's really at stake, quite simply, is the future of the family. When wedding-planning issues go unresolved, when mistakes are not forgiven, and when decisions lead to resentment, future issues become harder to deal with.

Take the common problem of divorced parent(s) who are not talking to each other and may refuse to be in each other's presence at the wedding. Because they are so entrenched in an adversarial situation, the bride and groom are placed in an impossible situation, having to choose between the two parents (and potentially stepparents). Situations like these involving the same people will happen repeatedly, and similar situations involving different people will require the same skills to address.

But that's just the beginning. The same choices facing the now-married couple will happen again when they start a family. They will have to decide whom to invite to birthday celebrations, Thanksgiving, Christmas, baptisms, First Communions, Mother's Day, Father's Day, and so on. Mistakes involving whom you invite to these post-wedding events often have short- and long-term effects.

Not inviting certain people such as children or distant relatives can often result in resentment for long periods. Sometimes, it's not worth alienating relatives, who will be in your lives for a long time if you don't invite their children.

So, think carefully about these issues so that you have a loving relationship with friends and relatives for a long time. Here are seven areas in which you can develop superior life skills.

COLLABORATION

> Call to me and I will answer you, and will tell you great and hidden things that you have not known. (Jeremiah 33:3)

Collaboration usually leads to a more enjoyable and special ceremony and reception!

Combine all the experiences and skill sets you (the couple), your parents and grandparents, your siblings, and your friends have, and you have an immense pool of resources from which to draw and an incredible group of people who are happy to support you. For example, among the book's co-authors, we possess all these professional and personal skills:

- advertising, marketing, publishing
- research, writing, and proofreading
- planning and running events
- performing music with bands
- teaching and working with groups of people
- creating artistic design

Within our small group and based on these skills, we could and did help couples to:

- make suggestions about the choices of music
- design save-the-date cards, invitations, programs, table cards, sign-in boards, and even centerpieces
- be aware of aspects of the ceremony and reception that they may not have considered

Expressing your vision to your collaborators as early as possible will be extremely helpful to them (see chapter 1, "Having a Vision").

As we like to say, "When it comes to wedding planning and life, like sports and in business, teamwork makes the dream work." And collaboration includes all the following components.

COMPROMISE

> Those who are hot-tempered stir up strife, but those who are slow to anger calm contention. (Proverbs 15:18)

The ability to compromise for the better outcome in any situation involves:

- working as a team
- giving and taking—the essence of compromise
- listening with your full attention and considering what the other person wants
- considering the needs, wants, and happiness of the other person, and asking that they do the same when you make requests
- respecting and not judging others' perspectives, opinions, and feelings
- involving others, as much as possible, in making decisions

- being positive at all times in your discussions
- refraining from holding compromises over other people's heads
- embracing decisions, even if you don't agree, to avoid resentment

COMMUNICATION

They have lost all sensitivity and have abandoned themselves to licentiousness, greedy to practice every kind of impurity. (Ephesians 4:19)

Becoming a good communicator is essential, not only for wedding planning but also for daily living, and this includes the following key components:

- talking about your needs and desires openly, clearly, and honestly
- making no assumptions about what others may think or feel
- always being positive when communicating
- listening attentively and not judging the opinions of others
- not interrupting others and derailing effective communication
- expressing what is important to you
- repeating what you've heard to confirm what is intended
- not dredging up the past in current conversations
- not using sarcasm or other negative expressions
- only stating your opinion; not referencing others to support your case

ADVERSITY

Set your heart right and be steadfast, and do not be impetuous in time of calamity. (Ben Sira 2:2)

Dealing with different types of adversity and personalities that clash with yours is something to master now, as they always enter relationships. Specifically, you must:

- understand that success in any relationship is often hard work
- be realistic about the constant adjustments to change and problems that arise
- adjust to major events—job change, sickness, marriage, children, death, accidents, major purchases, and so on
- communicate effectively during hard times to draw closer to each other, family, and friends
- draw on the power of prayer to help you through adversity
- face hardships together instead of alone
- have everyone recognize their part in facing any difficulty to achieve positive outcomes
- seek guidance from those you trust to deal with adversity
- find a combination of time, consistent hard work, and prayer to stay calm

REACTING TO OTHERS

Above all, maintain constant love for one another, for love covers a multitude of sins. (1 Peter 4:8)

How you react to others in adversarial situations often sets the tone for the outcome of the conflict. Be aware of the following time-tested truths:

- Understand that it takes longer to think through an issue than feel an emotional response.
- Practice a well-thought-out action instead of a quick reaction.
- Do not allow emotions to rule your responses.
- Always think carefully before you speak.
- Empathize with people during difficult discussions.
- Validate other people's experiences—"Yes, I hear you and understand what you're saying."

PERFECTION

(For the law made nothing perfect); there is, on the other hand, the introduction of a better hope, through which we approach God. (Hebrews 7:19)

There's rarely a need to become obsessed with perfection (see chapter 2). Consider the following:

- Chasing perfection is always difficult and in many cases not worth the effort.
- Aiming for perfection takes time and energy away from other things.
- It's easy to fall into the "perfection trap" when something less is just as good.
- No human being is perfect, so it's unrealistic to expect perfection.

DON'T SWEAT THE SMALL STUFF

Do not worry about anything, but in everything by prayer and supplication with thanksgiving let your requests be made known to God. (Philippians 4:6)

There's a reason that clichés like "don't sweat the small stuff" endure, and that's because they are true. Here's our take:

- With so many big things that happen in life, spending time on the small things is often destructive and a waste of time.
- Make quick decisions about small stuff. For example, do you really need to agonize over the color of napkins or who takes out the trash?
- Put things into perspective. Will spending a lot of time on any given issue be of significance in the grand scheme of things?
- Forgive your spouse and others who make a big deal of the small stuff.
- Focus on the positive aspects of any specific issue.
- Avoid worrying. It is better to act than worry.
- When something happens in your life, ask yourself if it will matter in a year, five years, or ten years from now.
- Make a commitment to yourself to not sweat the small stuff unless you honestly believe that specific small things are worth the effort to resolve.

Now you have a roadmap to enjoy loving, healthy, and stress-free relationships as you start married life. Refer to specific sections of this book as situations arise that need to be addressed. And above all, enjoy your family life together!

Final Thoughts

Peg Hensler

You may not know this, but the Catholic Church works closely with newly engaged couples, playing a major role in assuring they will have the best possible marriage. If you want a Catholic wedding, take advantage of what is intended as a cornerstone of your local parish life, one that provides you with a wealth of information and welcomes you into a caring and nurturing local community.

In countless conversations with deacons, priests, and laypeople who work with couples, one "almost always true" sentiment emerges: couples that take the time and make the effort to embrace the Catholic approach to marriage are way better off than those who don't.

In my thirty-five years of working with engaged couples, I know for sure that couples who make their marriage preparation a priority and who rely on the ongoing support of their Catholic faith community have happier and healthier marriages.

So, with that in mind, use this guidebook often throughout the wedding planning process, and above all, enjoy your big day in the Catholic way!

About the Authors

Irv Brechner has authored twenty-seven books, including the bestsellers *The College Survival Kit* and *The Career Finder*. His wife, **Nadine Brechner**, has planned hundreds of highly successful events. Nadine and Irv's daughter, Stephanie, married Patrick in October 2020 in front of 35 people (due to COVID-19) and celebrated their marriage the following October, witnessed by 120 people. "The two most important ways to resolve issues are for everyone to listen carefully to others and to compromise. It works!" says Irv.

Peg Hensler is a parish catechetical leader who served as the associate director for Marriage Ministries and Natural Family Planning (NFP) in the Diocese of Trenton, New Jersey, from 2004 until recently. She and her husband of nearly forty years, Bob Hensler, have served together in various marriage-related ministries since 1987 and have helped prepare countless couples for Catholic marriage. Peg and Bob have led retreats for married couples for various dioceses across the country.

Peg is a graduate of St. Joseph's University, Philadelphia, and completed her graduate work at LaSalle University with a master's degree in theology and ministry. She has served as a board member for the National Association of Catholic Family Life Ministers and as president of the New Jersey Council of Family Life Directors.

Peg and Bob reside in Haddon Township, New Jersey, and are active members of their local Catholic parish. Their greatest joy is spending time with their three adult children and son-in-law, and most especially their beloved grandchildren, Tilly and Benny.

Paulette and John Pitonyak's son, JP, married Sabrina in October 2021. Because of the required distance that was necessary during the pandemic, they delayed the wedding but started planning a year in advance, with the couple taking the lead.

They all agreed that "good relationships fostered before planning enabled everyone to have great communications and enjoy every step along the way."

Paulette and John attended seventeen weddings in a three-year period, and although the majority of brides and grooms were Catholic, none had a Catholic marriage ceremony. This provided the impetus for John to contact Peg Hensler in the hopes that this book would promote more Catholic marriages.

Due to the pandemic, **Carol and Bob Schilling**'s daughter, Jennifer, married Matthew in October 2020, witnessed by 30 close family and friends. They renewed their vows and celebrated their marriage the following year in October 2021 before 180 guests.

Carol and Bob say, "Talk to each other and always find the humor!"

After a thirty-year teaching career, Paulette, with Carol, wrote and illustrated five children's books that were inspired by Carol's grandniece.